Additional Praise for *The Hedge Fund Book*

"Those new to the hedge fund industry will benefit immensely from the chapter devoted to answering frequently asked question about hedge funds as well as the easy-to-understand explanations of all major areas of hedge funds throughout the book. Experienced hedge fund professionals reading this book will also gain valuable insight from other managers and service providers on current issues facing hedge funds. Whether you are looking to raise more capital, improve your fund's operations and due diligence, launch a new hedge fund, or just learn more about hedge funds, this book is a must-read."

— **Theo O'Brien**, Associate, Private Equity Investment Group

"Richard's new book is a terrific testament to the knowledge that he and his team have of the hedge fund industry. From novice to expert hedgers, I recommend this training manual. Its information makes for a sharp, timely evaluation of where hedge funds are and where they are likely to be heading."

— **Thomas J. Powell**, CEO, ELP Capital Advisers, Inc; Author, *Standing in the Rain: Understanding, Surviving and Thriving in the Worst Financial Storm since the Great Depression.*

"Richard Wilson is the best single source for practical answers on the hedge fund industry. For people new to the industry or considering launching their own fund, look no further. You'll find it all here."

— **Richard Zahm**, Portfolio Manager, Second Angel Fund I

"This book caters to hedge fund aspirants as well as finance professionals. Richard does a wonderful job of demystifying any misconceptions that the hedge fund industry faces today. Through a combination of interviews with industry professionals, a top down approach to both the basic and more complex nuances of running a hedge fund and colorful examples of the industry, Richard has been able to achieve what so many other hedge fund books aspire to. To capture the reader in both an enjoyable and informative book that will soon become a standard in the finance education industry."

— **Curtis Birchall**, Longbow Capital, Inc.

"*The Hedge Fund Book* provides an "inside baseball" look at the hedge fund industry and should be required reading for someone looking to get into the business."

— **Scott Freund**, Senior Family Wealth Advisor, GCC Family Wealth Management

"I wish this book had been around when we got started. This piece accelerates the ramping up period for hedge fund management company founders and executives. Most people think that to have a hedge fund all you need is a good trader and a Bloomberg terminal. They are shocked when they learn what it really takes to be successful. This book does a phenomenal job of explaining and exploring these keys to success."
—**Pratik Sharma**, Hedge Fund Manager

"*The Hedge Fund Book* is one of the few books that specifically address the "business" of hedge funds. Make no mistake, running a hedge fund is a business just like any brick and mortar store that requires attention to operations, sales and marketing, compliance, etc. as well as investment returns. Now more then ever, institutional investors are placing an emphasis on back/middle office functions. *The Hedge Fund Book* offers practical insight and advice from seasoned professionals on these overlooked aspects of a hedge fund business."
—**Nakul Nayyar**, U.S. Long/Short Hedge Fund Trader

"*The Hedge Fund Book: A Training Manual for Professional and Capital Raising Executives* by Richard Wilson is an excellent guide for established and developing hedge fund managers, and can be used as a point of reference in the administration of best practices of hedge funds and investor relations."
—**Valerie Emanuel**, President, Valerie Emanuel & Associates

The Hedge Fund Book

*A Training Manual
for Professionals and
Capital-Raising Executives*

RICHARD C. WILSON

WILEY

John Wiley & Sons, Inc.

Published by John Wiley & Sons, Inc., Hoboken, New Jersey.
Published simultaneously in Canada.

For general information on our other products and services or for technical support, please contact our Customer Care Department within the United States at (800) 762-2974, outside the United States at (317) 572-3993 or fax (317) 572-4002.

Wiley also publishes its books in a variety of electronic formats. Some content that appears in print may not be available in electronic books. For more information about Wiley products, visit our web site at www.wiley.com.

Library of Congress Cataloging-in-Publication Data:

Wilson, Richard C.
  The hedge fund book : a training manual for professionals and capital-raising executives / Richard Wilson.
      p. cm. – (Wiley finance series)
  Includes index.
  ISBN 978-0-470-52063-5 (cloth)
  1. Hedge funds.   I. Title.
  HG4530.W546 2010
  332.64'524–dc22
                                                                                2010003434

Printed in the United States of America.

10 9 8 7 6 5 4 3 2 1

This book is dedicated to my wife, Adriana Wilson, for being a wonderful person and a constant balancing force in my life. Despite my passion for business and marketing, the Brazilian in her makes sure that on some level I work to live and not live to work.

Contents

Preface

This book was created as a training manual for professionals who work in the hedge fund industry or who would like to work more closely with hedge funds as clients or business partners. Over the past seven years I have read most of the hedge fund books that are available. There are great books on hedge fund investment strategies, the history of hedge funds, financial modeling, and risk management. I never could find a book, though, that provided unfiltered advice, insights, and hard lessons learned from hedge fund managers. This gap in the marketplace and the growing needs of our Certified Hedge Fund Professional (CHP) Designation program is what led to this book being created.

Within this book, I hope that every reader will learn:

- How hedge fund managers of any hedge fund may increase their operational effectiveness immediately.
- Why most hedge fund managers struggle to raise capital, and how being proactive within the right areas can allow a small team to raise a large amount of capital.
- How to implement governance best practices that will improve investor confidence, enhance decision-making processes, and decrease the risk of some types of fraud.
- How to emulate the best practices of $1 billion-plus giant hedge funds that have learned many lessons the hard way.
- Why what you read about hedge funds in the general media is off-base 80 percent of the time.
- How to double the effectiveness of your capital-raising efforts by focusing on your unique process and positioning more than on your numbers.
- How small to medium-size hedge funds in the real world are improving their business structure and processes without spending millions on infrastructure.

The intended audience for this book includes CHP Designation participants, hedge fund managers, professors, traders, third-party marketers, students, service providers, investors, and consultants. The book provides a fundamental understanding of how hedge funds operate at a high level, while also taking the reader down to very granular, real-world steps that hedge fund managers can take to improve how they manage risk, operate, select service providers, govern their own organization, and raise capital. This text should help readers shortcut the process of interviewing 30 hedge fund managers and veterans, by providing their advice, tips, strategies, and painful lessons learned here within one concise book. If you add up all the time of the managers and consultants who were involved within these interviews, the book contains over $80,500 worth of advice yet costs less than $75.

In addition to the chapters of the book that focus on niche subjects such as institutionalization, capital raising, governance, or best practices of $1 billion-plus hedge funds, this book contains multimedia resources that should help the reader comprehend and absorb the advice provided herein. We have created over 50 video and audio resources, which you will see referenced through this book. These may be used to supplement university course lectures or sent to team members who may also want to learn more about hedge funds and how they operate. To access these resources, please visit HedgeFundTraining.com.

MY STORY

To provide some background as to why this book was written, here's a short explanation of how I entered the hedge fund industry. My first experience in working with hedge funds was in 2001 when I completed an internship for a currency/commodity-based hedge fund in Europe. I helped them complete leading-indicator trading research on the currencies and commodities of Japan, New Zealand, and Australia and analyzed the relationships between them.

After completing this work, I started learning more about marketing and sales and found myself drawn more to finding out how to raise capital and connect with investors. This led me to independently negotiate and sign contracts to raise capital for a boutique investment bank in New York and one of the early fund of hedge funds groups based out of South Africa. I helped them raise capital by identifying potential institutional investors, completing market research, and reaching out to investors.

After working within this area while also consulting within the area of risk management for three years, I took a position with a third-party marketing firm. This firm raised capital for three to five fund clients at a time, and I was in charge of completing the hands-on marketing of three clients: an $80 billion long-only portfolio optimization firm, a $30 million U.S. hedge fund manager, and an $800 million global macro hedge fund manager. This unique set of clients and my responsibilities of researching new potential investors, building organic investor databases, e-mailing investors, completing educational marketing, calling investors, working conferences, and creating marketing materials taught me a lot about how things should and should not be done. In this role I raised a depressing $0 the first 11 months, and then started raising $100,000 a week. Eventually, after 18 months, raising a minimum of $1 million to $3 million a week.

While marketing these funds, I found that due to the fragmented structure of the industry, most fund marketers simply follow their competitors' strategies. In addition, most have few resources to leverage, focus little on positioning, complete no capital-raising training, and ignore the power of writing strong copy and using educational approaches to marketing to investors. At the same time, my online networking association, the Hedge Fund Group, grew to over 30,000 members and my blog, HedgeFundBlogger.com, was taking off and quickly became the number one most widely visited web site on hedge funds.

I decided to fly solo and start my own firm in 2008. We now run three main product and service lines:

1. Our training programs such as the CHP Designation, Hedge Fund Startup Kit, and Hedge Fund Marketing Mechanics hedge funds
2. Our blog network on hedge funds, private equity, mutual funds, alternative investments and capital raising where we provide over 5,000 original articles, videos, and interviews
3. Our capital-raising tools and investor databases, which have now been used by over 1,600 fund managers and include HedgeFundDirectoryPro.com, HedgeFundInvestorDirectory.com, PrivateEquityDirectory.com, Investor Databases.com, and CapitalRaiserPro.com

Our firm and team are small but growing. We have a total of 25 full- and part-time employees and contractors now who help us offer and constantly update the CHP Designation, blogs, and these capital-raising tools.

DISCLOSURE OF FINANCIAL INTERESTS

In the spirit of transparency and full disclosure which I recommend within this text, I think it is only appropriate to disclose my own interests. I was only able to write this book based on my current relationships, consulting projects, capital-raising experience, and services that my firm offers. Because of this, there are overlaps between examples in this book and my own clients and products. For example, I have asked my closest circle of 30 or so clients to review my book for feedback or a quote. Also, three out of the 25 professionals I interviewed within this book have used my consulting services in the past, and my firm has financial interests and/or ownership in the following web sites and resources mentioned within the rest of this book: CHP Designation (HedgeFundCertification.com), InvestorDatabases .com, HedgeFundInvestorDirectory.com, PrimeBrokerageGuide.com, Third PartyMarketing.com, HedgeFundBlogger.com, HedgeFundStartupGuru .com, ThirdPartyMarketing.com, HedgeFundsBook.com, HedgeFund Premium.com, and FamilyOfficesDatabase.com. My hope is that the over 250 hours of consulting advice and over 50 video modules within this book are worth far more than any distraction by the handful of mentions of the web sites or services that we provide.

Acknowledgments

Thank you to my father, Thomas Wilson, for pushing me to write my first "real book" based on the consulting, marketing, and writing I have already done. Thank you to my wife, Adriana, for patiently supporting me in everything we have been aiming to accomplish. Thank you to Jonathan King, who woke me up and spurred me to stop floating through business, to take control of where I was headed, and to work toward something greater than average.

Also, a quick thank-you to someone who is probably too busy to ever read this sentence: Jeffrey Gitomer. If it were not for the inspiration obtained through his writing, I would have never learned to kick my own or started a blog, newsletter, or book. My constant push to give away more writing and free educational materials can be attributed directly to Gitomer.

Above all else, thank you to the more than 900,000 professionals who have e-mailed our team, downloaded our free hedge fund blog book, completed our CHP Designation hedge fund training program, and used our capital, raising resources. Your support, loyalty, and feedback are what drove me to publish this text, and have been the source of ideas for every product and service we offer. Thank you for sharing your time and thoughts with me.

Introduction

What if you sat down with 30 hedge fund veterans and picked their brains? What if you spent over $80,000 hiring professionals with seven to 30 or more years of experience to provide you their insights on what is developing in the hedge fund industry, and what is important now?

This is the premise on which I constructed *The Hedge Fund Book: A Training Manual for Professionals and Capital-Raising Executives.*

This book is a discussion, a captured forum, not a dissertation, letter to Congress, or formal legal document. You will find less formality here than in most books, because that is how I am used to writing and transferring knowledge through speeches, e-mails, and blog posts. Some may appreciate this approach and form of communication; others will surely not.

The Hedge Fund Book: A Training Manual for Professionals and Capital-Raising Executives will provide many benefits to those seeking to understand and work in this field. Our team at the Hedge Fund Group has raised millions of dollars of capital for hedge funds and personally worked with over 1,000 fund managers over the past several years. In the past we have freely shared our knowledge through our blogs, which you may still access today. They include:

- HedgeFundBlogger.com
- HedgeFundsCareer.com
- ThirdPartyMarketing.com
- FamilyOfficesGroup.com
- HedgeFundStartupGuru.com
- CommoditiesAndFuturesGuide.com
- PrimeBrokerageGuide.com
- PrivateEquityBlogger.com

In addition to the more than 10,000 articles provided in these blogs, our free e-book has also been downloaded more than 100,000 times. These articles and resources were given away freely to develop relationships with those who found value in the resources.

In an effort to now make this book worth more than the retail price, we include many diverse types of educational resources including case studies,

1

examples, interviews, best practices, review questions, and video resources to help readers learn more about hedge funds. These interviews and videos were produced by hedge fund principals and consultants who normally either do not provide such advice or typically charge $200 to $475 per hour for their time. My hope is that the value of these additional resources alone will be worth more than what you paid to obtain this book. If you add up the 250-plus hours that went into putting this book together with all of the experienced professionals we interviewed, there is more than $80,500 worth of advice contained in this text. Here are some more details on the different resources included in this text and how they operate:

- *Interviews.* Over 20 interviews complete this training manual for the hedge fund industry, including many of the full transcripts in this text. The advice comes directly from numerous veterans in the industry, so individual readers do not need to interview all of them directly.
- *Video resources.* We have also created a series of over 40 video resources which act as a supplement to this training manual. Throughout this book there are references to specific video resources, and the complete list of videos available may be seen at http://HedgeFundTraining.com/Videos.
- *Frequently asked questions.* Our team at the Hedge Fund Group has received and sent over 800,000 e-mails since our firm was started in 2007. We have received thousands of e-mails on capital raising, starting a hedge fund, institutionalization, and hedge fund careers. I have used about 40 of the most frequent of these questions to create Chapter 9 of this book. Some professionals may find this resource more valuable than the rest of the chapter-by-chapter instruction and interview content.
- *Why important.* Each chapter begins with a short section on why the chapter is critical to the health and growth of the hedge fund as a business. This provision guides the reader as to which chapters will be most relevant to his particular career or business.
- *Chapter review questions.* Each chapter concludes with several review questions for those professors and trainers who have agreed to use this manual as part of their university course. These will also be helpful for those who are completing the hedge fund training and certification program referred to in this text as the Certified Hedge Fund Professional (CHP) Designation Program (www.HedgeFundCertification.com).

I recently participated in a training session with Eben Pagan in Los Angeles at a marketing conference on how business is typically conducted. He told an interesting story. Eben spoke about how the streets in Boston are actually old cow paths that the city decided to just pave over to create the roads of the city. The result is a very complicated maze of one-way streets that really only make sense to the most veteran cab drivers. This is not the cows' fault. They simply walked typically in the direction of least resistance. Nobody stepped back and looked at where the cows had wandered and asked if there was a better way to get the project done—they simply followed where cows had walked in the past.

Eben's point in telling this story was that in every business, every form of marketing, and even in the hedge fund business, there are cow paths everywhere. The question is whether you and your business are wandering around on the cow paths of what others have done in the past, or building a super highway straight toward your goal.

Areas to examine for hedge fund managers could include hiring, capital raising, employee management, performance reporting, transparency, governance, and investor relations. It helps to step back and look at competitors, other industries, and steps needed to complete the work we are trying to complete, to see if there is a more direct or efficient way of fully accomplishing it.

 BONUS VIDEO MODULE

To watch a video on hedge fund cow paths, please type this URL into your Web browser: http://HedgeFundTraining.com/Cow

CHAPTER 1

Hedge Fund Fundamentals

Training is everything. The peach was once a bitter almond;
cauliflower is nothing but cabbage with a college education.
                                                                    —Mark Twain

T his chapter provides a brief 20,000-foot-view introduction to hedge funds
  and provides a context for the content of this book. In this chapter I briefly
cover the history of hedge funds, important definitions, the hedge fund
ecosystem, media portrayal of hedge funds, five industry trends, regulations,
and the future of hedge funds.

Why important: This chapter is the foundation for the rest of this book.
If you have more than five years of industry experience, you may want to
skim this chapter and skip to the chapter review questions to check your
level of industry knowledge.

What this chapter is not: This book is not a thorough review of hedge
fund investment strategies or analytics; those topics are already covered in
dozens of other texts, including two that are required in the Certified Hedge
Fund Professional (CHP) Designation Program. See these required books
and other recommendations at HedgeFundBookstore.com.

What *is* a hedge fund? The one-sentence definition of a hedge fund is
"a private investment vehicle that charges its investors two types of fees: a
management fee and a performance fee." Any more specific definition will
lead to conflicts in the industry today, as it has grown in many directions.
The management fee is a standard fee based on total assets under management and it typically runs between 1 and 2 percent. The second type of fee
typically charged by hedge funds is a performance fee; typically this is 10 to
20 percent and is charged based on the performance achieved by the fund.
If a hedge fund has 10 percent positive performance for a single year and its
performance fee is 20 percent, the hedge fund's management would get to

keep 2 percent of that 10 percent gain as part of their profits, a reward for achieving these positive returns for their investors.

 BONUS VIDEO MODULE

Watch a video explaining what a hedge fund is and is not, here: HedgeFundTraining.com/What-is-a-Hedge-Fund?

HEDGE FUND MECHANICS AND STATISTICS

It is important to know that while these fee figures just mentioned are typical, the hedge fund industry has become competitive and diverse. There are now hedge funds operating that charge a 0 percent management fee while others charge 3 percent. Wide variations in performance fee levels may also be seen. One important aspect of this dual-level fee structure is the incentive it sets in place for hedge fund managers. While many hedge fund managers have already invested their own assets in the portfolio they are managing, remunerating the managers based on positive performance and not just total assets under management rewards those who can achieve consistent year-after-year gains. This in turn leads to rich compensation for those who can outperform the majority, and it attracts the best of talent to the industry. A portfolio manager can potentially earn two to three times as much working for a hedge fund as he could working for a similar size mutual fund or long-only optimization firm.

Investments made in hedge funds are typically seen as medium to long term for several reasons. The main reason is liquidity. Most hedge funds have lock-up periods of one to two years, and many restrict redemptions for as long as three years after the initial investment is made. A lock-up period simply means that the investor may not redeem his invested funds until this period has expired. These lock-up periods are put into place so that the hedge fund may invest in various assets and will have more control and flexibility in the timing of its purchasing and selling of these assets over time. Without lock-up periods, a manager may make a long-term investment in a security, for example, and a new investor could come and request his assets back during a weak point in the markets, forcing the manager to sell the security at a loss to meet that redemption request. While lock-up periods help managers in running their funds, they are seen as a major concern and drawback by institutions and high net worth (HNW) investors. While this book does not cover hedge fund replication or publicly traded hedge funds, these are two areas worth additional research if this topic is of interest to the reader.

There are between 100,000 and 150,000 professionals who work directly within the hedge fund industry and another 1,000,000-plus professionals who work with hedge funds in some way, indirectly or as part of a broader platform of services. There are between 10,000 and 25,000 hedge funds in existence today, depending on whose statistics and databases you trust most, and new funds are launched daily. The average hedge fund has just around $40 million in assets under management (AUM), while many start with just $500,000 to $5 million, and a larger group runs over $1 billion in assets.

 BONUS VIDEO MODULE

To watch a video on hedge fund liquidity and lock-up periods, please type this URL into your Web browser: http://HedgeFundTraining.com/Liquidity

Additional Common Hedge Fund Terms

- *Hurdle rate*: A hurdle rate is a set performance figure that must be achieved before any performance fees will be calculated or paid to the hedge fund manager. For example, a hedge fund may have its hurdle rate set at 3 percent so that any performance above 3 percent will be considered outperformance. Hurdle rates avoid having investors pay high fees for low-single-digit portfolio performance.

 BONUS VIDEO MODULE

To watch a video on the definition of a hurdle rate, please type this URL into your Web browser: http://HedgeFundTraining.com/Hurdle

- *High-water mark*: A high-water mark is a tool by which hedge fund managers can assure investors that they will not be charged performance fees after portfolio losses until the fund has made up those past losses. In other words, if a hedge fund manager has a loss of 5 percent in one year, he may not be paid any performance fees in the following year until he has first regained that loss, restoring the fund to the high-water mark point. Again, the high-water mark protects investors from paying the performance fee until the manager has made up the ground he previously lost in the portfolio.

BONUS VIDEO MODULE

To watch a video on the definition of a high-water mark, please type this URL into your Web browser: http://HedgeFundTraining.com/ High

- *Gating clause:* A gating clause allows a hedge fund manager, under certain circumstances, to restrict or completely cut off redemptions from the portfolio due to market illiquidity or specific sets of circumstances set forth in the contract. This term has been highly debated recently due to hundreds of funds "closing the gate" or enacting this clause in their agreements with investors.

For more definitions, please see the Glossary at the back of this book.

HISTORY OF HEDGE FUNDS

Financial journalist, author, and sociologist Alfred W. Jones started the first hedge fund in 1949 while working for *Fortune*. The fund was started on the belief that the movements of individual securities were due to both the performance of that specific security and the performance of the broader markets. His strategy was to address this by investing in securities that seemed to be positioned to outperform the market, while *shorting* (see Glossary) or selling those securities that seemed likely to underperform the market. The goal was to neutralize or cancel out market risk by allowing the portfolio to hedge against negative market movements. This is how the first hedge fund was created. This idea was unique in that it was designed to do well, or at least relatively well, during volatile or even bear market conditions.

This new method of managing portfolios of equities started becoming popular in the 1960s, and by the 1970s there were over 150 hedge funds in existence managing close to $1 billion in assets. Some early hedge fund managers were Warren Buffett, Michael Steinhardt, and George Soros. Since then hedge funds have evolved to include commodities, bonds, real estate, and other types of assets.

Over time, the term *hedge fund* took on the broader definition of a general private investment partnership, which typically includes management and performance fees as the only common denominator. Even this definition is now becoming dated as more hedge funds and firms that run hedge funds become publicly traded companies. Hedge funds are hard to understand as a whole because they are diverse and somewhat secretive. Hedge funds are secretive because of strict advertising and public offering rules as well as to keep their investment process, trading strategy, and positions from their competition. The hedge fund industry is very competitive and entrepreneurial.

 BONUS VIDEO MODULE

To watch a video on the history of the hedge fund industry, please type this URL into your Web browser: http://HedgeFundTraining.com/History

MEDIA PORTRAYAL OF HEDGE FUNDS

Along the way there have been hedge fund blowups (that have had performance dives and made public headlines), fraud cases, insider trading, and misreporting. While the whole idea of what a hedge fund does has been growing, public knowledge of these vehicles is still relatively limited and misunderstood, and hedge funds are often in the bottom 1 percent of the industry in terms of ethics or performance that makes the headlines each day. Hedge funds are now mentioned in thousands of magazines and newspapers each month.

There are often misconceptions formed about hedge funds, which are largely caused by reading mainstream news sources on the topic. Here are the top three misconceptions caused by the media:

1. Hedge funds are large multibillion-dollar investment vehicles that can destroy companies. *Reality*: While the largest of hedge funds do control

a large share of total assets under management, the industry is actually made up of mostly $1 million to $200 million size hedge fund managers.

2. Hedge funds are not regulated. *Reality*: Many hedge funds are already regulated at the asset level based on what they are investing in.

3. Hedge funds are always committing fraud and blowing up their funds. *Reality*: Less than 0.1 percent of the industry is ever accused of any fraud claims, and a 2006 study by Capco shows that over half of all hedge fund failures are actually due to operational business reasons and not performance-related issues.

 BONUS VIDEO MODULE

To watch a video called "Media Portrayal of Hedge Funds: Misconceptions and Myths," please type this URL into your Web browser: http://HedgeFundTraining.com/Media

HEDGE FUND ECOSYSTEM

Hedge fund managers do not work in a vacuum where they coordinate directly with investors and receive no assistance from outside parties. Most hedge fund managers work with at least three of the five types of service providers shown in Figure 1.1.

It is important to know the function of each of these parties to understand how hedge funds operate, and how they invest and control their assets. Here are definitions and explanations for each of these service provider types:

1. *Prime brokerage.* Prime brokers provide a package of services typically within the largest business of an investment bank. The following services are sometimes offered by prime brokers: custody, securities lending, financing, customized technology, operational support, capital introduction, and other trading-related services.

2. *Fund administration.* Fund administration firms provide support and operational services to hedge fund managers. These services may include accounting services, operational/finance services, settlement of daily trades, calculation and payment of distributions, and payment of fund expenses.

FIGURE 1.1   Types of Service Providers Used by Hedge Funds

3. *Third Party marketing.* Third party marketing firms are independent hedge fund marketing consultants who work to raise capital for two to five or more hedge funds at any one point in time for a single source of investors, or for multiple distribution channels. They typically require some sort of retainer along with sharing of 20 percent of both the management and performance fees while the funds raised stay invested.
4. *Legal and compliance.* Legal and compliance firms become more important every year within the hedge fund industry. Hedge funds use law firms for complicated formation processes, ongoing business legal considerations, and ongoing compliance work as well.
5. *Auditing.* Auditing firms are used by hedge funds on a quarterly and annual basis to verify their performance and accounting figures. Some hedge funds use auditing firms for monthly checks or to prepare for an annual audit as well.

 BONUS VIDEO MODULE

To watch a video on the hedge fund ecosystem, please type this URL into your Web browser: http://HedgeFundTraining.com/Ecosystem

Top Four Hedge Fund Industry Trends

Understanding the hedge fund industry requires knowing what is going on now and also identifying current trends affecting how hedge funds operate, invest, form, and trade. Following are the top four hedge fund industry trends:

1. Recent poor absolute hedge fund performance and fraud has led to increasing pressure from investors for additional transparency and levels of governance. This is being done to ensure that managers adhere to their investment mandates, only restrict investor liquidity when necessary, and ensure that internal controls, checks, and responsibilities are properly carried out. Independent administration firms and directors are now required by many investors and boards of advisers.

2. The collapse of Lehman Brothers left some hedge funds in London without access to their assets, causing poor performance and in some cases fund failures. Since this event, hedge funds with over $30 million in assets have been investigating and implementing multi–prime brokerage models, rather than invite risk by working with one single prime broker. In the past, prime brokerage firms would conduct due diligence on the soundness of their potential hedge fund clients. Now the research is done in both directions, with hedge funds screening prime brokers and vice versa. Some newcomers to the industry are now gaining strong market share because they are seen as a safe place to do business.

3. The use of outside capital-raising resources, investor databases, and third-party marketing firms is on the rise. The capital-raising environment is more competitive, and hedge fund managers are forced to evolve their investor relationship cultivation systems, capital introduction resources, and investor contacts in order to compete.

4. Investors increasingly want to work with more *institutional* hedge fund managers. This typically means hedge funds with over $100 million to $250 million in assets under management. More specifically, it refers to the types of operational processes, technology, risk management, trading, and governance features that tend to be in place with funds that have $1 billion in assets under management. This has always been a challenge for emerging managers, who have limited access to high-pedigree (well respected and accomplished) team members, investors comfortable with small fund managers, and many times even the knowledge needed to create a more institutional-quality hedge fund operation.

BONUS VIDEO MODULE

To watch a video on the top four hedge fund trends, please type this URL into your Web browser: http://HedgeFundTraining.com/Trends

FUTURE OF THE HEDGE FUND INDUSTRY

During the financial crisis of 2008, many journalists wrote about the death of hedge funds and how the industry was about to burn to the ground. This was taken seriously by only a handful of professionals who actually worked in the industry. The future of the hedge fund industry is actually bright due to several short- and long-term factors.

The strongest argument for the strength of the hedge fund industry is the constant innovation that occurs in this industry. Hedge funds are constantly using new trading techniques, incorporating new asset classes, including additional equity markets in their scope, and taking on new financing and investing roles to expand their total market share. Most hedge funds on the edge of innovation are small, hungry teams that are driven to succeed, and they know that they will be rewarded handsomely for doing so. The combination of relatively low barriers of entry and direct financial rewards are a formula for continued growth and natural positive evolution of the industry as a whole.

 BONUS VIDEO MODULE

To watch a video on the future of the hedge fund industry, please see http://HedgeFundTraining.com/Future

CHAPTER SUMMARY

Hedge funds have been growing rapidly over the past 20 years, and while their growth is now slowing down, they are becoming more diverse and innovative in their investment strategies. As the industry evolves, service providers are becoming more like business partners and are vital to the business success of hedge fund managers. In the future, hedge funds are likely to develop even more investment terms, investor agreements, and performance fee structures to further align the interests of the investor with the hedge fund portfolio manager and principal.

Free Resource: The Free Hedge Fund E-Book, at HedgeFundsBook.com.

REVIEW QUESTIONS

1. What is a hedge fund?
   a. A private investment partnership that typically includes the manager of the portfolio receiving both a management and performance fee.
   b. A private equity fund that also employs hedging tactics using equity securities.
   c. A private investment partnership that is 100 percent unregulated and can use leverage to produce higher absolute returns for investors.
   d. The roles of the specific board members.
2. Which of the following is not one of the top trends affecting the hedge fund industry right now?
   a. Investors are seeking to work with more institutional-quality fund managers.
   b. Raising capital is becoming more competitive, so utilizing resources such as third-party marketers and investor databases is on the rise.
   c. Most hedge fund managers are now outsourcing their portfolio management activities to leading mutual funds, who trade the actual account in the hedge fund.
   d. Fund administrators, prime brokerage firms, compliance firms, third party marketers, and auditing firms are becoming increasingly important to the operations and effectiveness of a hedge fund business.
3. True or false: Due to the concentrated nature of hedge fund strategies, it is likely that another large market swing could eliminate the industry completely.
4. Hedge funds typically charge a _____ percent management fee and _____ percent performance fee.
   a. 3.5, 15
   b. 2, 25
   c. 1, 15
   d. 2, 20
5. True or false: A high-water mark allows a hedge fund manager, under certain circumstances, to restrict or completely cut off redemptions from

the portfolio due to market illiquidity or specific sets of circumstances set forth in the contract.

6. True or false: Hedge funds are the one type of investment that is completely unregulated, and that is why investment into this vehicle type is restricted to institutional and accredited investors.

7. Most of the hedge fund industry is made up of managers who manage between _____ and _____ in assets under management (AUM).
   a. $1 million, $10 million
   b. $100 million, $750 million
   c. $1 million, $200 million
   d. $50 million, $200 million

8. True or false: Financial journalist, author, and sociologist Andrew Lo started the first hedge fund in 1949 while working for *Fortune*.

9. A lock-up period is often put in place so that
   a. A hedge fund may invest in various assets and will have more control and flexibility in the timing of its purchasing and selling of these assets.
   b. A hedge fund may lock up an investor into investing only in its fund during a certain period of time, typically lasting 18 months to two years. This is put into place to protect the intellectual capital that may be shared with other managers in the industry.
   c. An investor can lock in his investment with the hedge fund and be guaranteed additional capacity in the hedge fund for the next two to three years after his initial investment. This is most commonly used by institutional investors.

10. True or false: Due to being highly liquid vehicles, hedge funds are often invested in for an average of six to nine weeks and offer liquidity on a weekly basis. This is why the industry has been able to quickly gain assets for institutional investors of many types.

Answers: To view the answers to these questions, please see http://HedgeFundTraining.com/Answers.

CHAPTER 2

Institutionalization and Operations

The most important contribution management needs to make in the twenty-first century is to increase the productivity of knowledge work and the knowledge worker.
—Peter F. Drucker

A study in 2006 by Capco shows that at least half of hedge fund failures are due to operational reasons rather than performance reasons. This runs contrary to what most would expect. To make matters more challenging, most fund managers come to the business with portfolio management or trading experience, not operational fund management experience. This chapter provides some operational best practices, tips, and recommendations from experts in the industry.

Why important: Everyone, including traders, service providers, marketers, and portfolio managers, contributes to the institutional processes and operations of a great hedge fund, and there are hundreds of tactics that may be employed as a fund's business grows. One thing is certain: If you are looking to grow your hedge fund to over $100 million in assets, not knowing how to improve the institutional quality of your hedge fund will result in a loss of assets to those who do understand and adapt to the institutional demands on hedge funds.

The hedge fund industry is becoming simultaneously more competitive and diverse. A fund manager starting business today will face more hurdles than any manager in the past in terms of regulations, objections, and gatekeepers. One of the most difficult ongoing challenges for managers from $1 million to $1 billion in assets under management (AUM) is the constant need to increase the institutional quality of the hedge fund's portfolio management, operations, marketing, and risk management. At the same time, most hedge fund managers have no mentor, mastermind group, or consistent help in becoming more institutional in how they operate. This chapter is meant to help fill that void in the industry and provide some tangible steps that managers can take to improve their processes and operations.

STEPHEN ABRAHAMS, VICE PRESIDENT OF MARKETING FOR A LONDON-BASED HEDGE FUND

Our first interview is with Stephen Abrahams, who has 20 years of financial advisory experience, from tied agent to index fund adviser (IFA) to offshore IFA, and has most recently been raising capital for a boutique hedge fund manager in London.

Richard Wilson: Stephen, from your experience in raising capital, what are the five top things that you believe hedge fund managers can do to become more institutional?

Stephen Abrahams: I believe that the top five things hedge funds managers can do would be:

1. Understand their strengths and weaknesses—know what their unique selling proposition (USP) really is.
2. Have better than average marketing materials and sale literature that is constructed by someone who knows what investors are looking for.
3. Employ an in-house salesman or hire a third-party marketer, or both. The managers can then concentrate on what they are good at by trading and managing the portfolio.
4. Take the long-term view and invest long-term; institutions take their time to make decisions.
5. Listen closely to objections, investor feedback, and clues to institutional checkboxes such as liquidity, size, transparency, and so on.

Richard Wilson: Great. That sounds like good advice. Many of the hedge fund managers I speak with are still trying to raise capital without any dedicated resource reaching out to new potential investors on a daily basis, and I always believe that is a mistake. It takes a concerted effort to grow assets in this competitive environment, and as you've suggested, this process can also help improve fund operations and positioning as an institutional quality fund. Many investors want to become more institutional to attract more capital to their funds. Is there any magic bullet that you have found to attract capital while you still have a small AUM?

Stephen Abrahams: Definitely not a magic bullet, as institutions have a tick-box mentality (very detailed, step-by-step checklist-type due diligence) and size does matter. You really need to have a set of contacts that look to invest in smaller funds to get you to that magic $100 million, which isn't easy and it takes a long time and a lot of hard work to accomplish.

Richard Wilson: I also liked two things you mentioned there, that there is no magic bullet, and "that magic $100 million" mark. I agree that there is no magic bullet in becoming more institutional or raising capital. It really does take day-after-day hard work and consistent, tenacious relationship development and adjustment of your marketing strategy. Also, while some research organizations might define emerging hedge funds as any funds with less than $250 million in AUM, in the real world 80 percent of the industry would consider a fund with over $100 million in AUM as coming out of the emerging manager zone.

I once had the fun job of calling every single institutional consulting firm in the United States—over 200 of them. At that time I was raising capital for a $600 million fund of hedge funds and a $10 million long/short fund. What I found was that over 95 percent of these consultants who represent large institutional investors require that you have $100 million or more in assets before they will seriously consider recommending you to their clients. In other words, they may complete some due diligence on you as an exercise or in anticipation that you may grow to over $100 million in size, but you won't get any real asset-growing traction with most of them until you get to that magic $100 million mark, as Stephen put it.

BOB PARDO, CEO AND PRESIDENT, PARDO CAPITAL LIMITED

Our next interview is with Bob Pardo of Pardo Capital Limited. Mr. Pardo has been a commodity trading adviser since 1996 and has worked with a wide variety of strategies, both short- and longer-term. Pardo Capital has an 11-year track record and has managed up to $50 million during operations, and they have picked up a lot of best practices along the way. Their investment strategies are based on their proprietary Walk-Forward Analysis methodology as described in Mr. Pardo's book, *The Evaluation and Optimization of Trading Strategies* (John Wiley & Sons, 2008).

Richard Wilson: What have you learned not to do, or what have you stopped doing related to trading or operations that was hurting your firm's position as a high-quality fund management business? Any lessons or tips to share on this point?

Bob Pardo: I would not say that we have stopped doing anything. I would say that we have reprioritized our research and development process to get viable products out there when they are in a form that is of interest to our investment space.

Richard Wilson: Besides AUM, what do you believe is most important for a hedge fund to focus on improving when thinking about institutionalizing a hedge fund? Risk management? Trading processes? Research? Pedigree?

Bob Pardo: It depends where the hedge fund is to start. They are all important. However, if you do not have a viable and competitive product, of course, you do not have a business. Assuming that, I would then rank pedigree, research, and infrastructure.

Richard Wilson: I agree, lots of times when professionals ask how they can raise $30 million for their hedge fund, the most honest response is "It depends." How has your firm gotten past the "under $100 million, no institutional quality operations" objection in the past? Gone to smaller investors who don't hold this objection? Met with investors face-to-face? Any lessons learned here?

Bob Pardo: The only real lesson to be learned here is the realization that with less than $100 million AUM, there are a lot of institutions of all types who will not be able to deal with you for a whole range of reasons. The flip side, then, is to identify and focus on those who will. Of course, there is the occasional opportunity to attract a $100 million investor and then just go on to the next stage of development.

Richard Wilson: What operational resources does your firm leverage or use to help outsource work or improve the efficiency of the work your fund faces to keep business moving forward each month?

Bob Pardo: We outsource a lot and it has its pros and cons. It is ideal for a small operation. At a certain size, however, a lot of outsourcing stops making sense. That being said, given the maturing of the entire space, outsourcing can often be done quite cost effectively.

Richard Wilson: I agree, every hedge fund I have ever worked with outsourced many functions. It almost never makes sense to do everything yourself, and on some level you simply can't while still offering a great product to your clients. Do your firm's marketers undergo formal capital raising or marketing training?

Bob Pardo: At this point, no. At the higher levels, we are interested in attracting proven talent. We feel that we can bring a lot to the table with our various types of expertise. At the level of newer talent, we prefer to groom in-house. In the end, after our intellectual property, our people are our number one resource. They represent stability and the potential for future growth

Richard Wilson: That will be refreshing for some young professionals to hear, who want to get into the industry. Many professionals who contact us regarding the CHP Designation have the view that if they didn't complete two or three hedge fund internships and obtain some sort of entry level hedge fund position in the past, there is not a whole lot of hope for them in the industry. I disagree, as there are many firms like yours who would like to train someone from the ground up.

Do you recommend that hedge fund start-ups begin raising capital from day 1, or are you in the camp that believes that a two- to four-year track record should be developed first?

Bob Pardo: Hit the ground running. We made the mistake of waiting, and aside from costing us a fortune in lost revenues, it hurt us in other ways as well. The industry has changed dramatically over the past several years. A two- to four-year track record is no longer a necessity in many cases. Pedigree and the proverbial "good story" carry a lot more weight these days.

Richard Wilson: I agree. There are two main reasons why I think it is never too early to begin marketing. First, a lot of business is done based on trust and relationships, so the earlier you start the stronger your relationships get. Second, by starting your marketing early, you move up the learning curve on what investors expect, what marketing materials need to be in place, and what resources may need to be dedicated to this type of work.

What is the critical issue that decides whether you work with a particular consultant, service provider, or marketer? What is the one thing that you always look for? Good service? Recommendations from others? Branding? Experience?

Bob Pardo: Experience and credibility and the ability for the service provider to demonstrate a track record, preferably, or a workable plan to provide the exact service that we need.

VINOD PAUL, MANAGING DIRECTOR OF SERVICE AND BUSINESS DEVELOPMENT, EZE CASTLE INTEGRATION

Our next interview is with Vinod Paul, managing director of service and business development at Eze Castle Integration, a leading and well-respected consulting and technology solutions firm which services hedge fund and investment firms. Leading a talented team of customer service and engineering professionals, Vinod Paul oversees all customer-facing engagements for Eze

Castle Integration. Vinod joined the company in 2002, and his responsibilities include service delivery and business development for the firm.

Richard Wilson: Vinod, what are some of the institutionalization and operational improvement trends that you are seeing with your hedge fund clients?

Vinod Paul: What I see is that they are reinvesting their tools. These start out as nice-to-haves and then turn into must-haves. An example of this is order management systems. Smaller firms with just one or two prime brokers do this in Excel, but as they grow past the $100 million they typically bring on prime broker numbers three, four, and five, and they need an order management system that fits their needs better. Other tools that were nice-to-haves and now are need-to-haves are customer relationship management (CRM) tools—they need this to manage investor reporting.

Richard Wilson: I have found that SalesForce.com is the most popular CRM tool for hedge funds today. What have you seen?

Vinod Paul: We see a variety and offer our own CRM solution. This is because we have about 650 hedge funds within our umbrella, and the issue with SalesForce.com is that it is very vanilla. It was not created for hedge funds and investment firms exclusively.

Richard Wilson: Are hedge funds missing the boat on operational best practices? Any advice?

Vinod Paul: The dynamics are changing. Hedge funds used to launch with little organization, wearing a lot of hats. In the past, compliance used to be half-done or outsourced, and this tool is very defined. Now there are multiple tools and guides and experts on what you should be doing each month and who should be doing it. There are now outsourcing services for this area, and this is a growing importance, so we are seeing a lot of firms invest up front in that now.

Richard Wilson: You work with literally hundreds of hedge funds who are always reinvesting in their infrastructure and operations. Any low-hanging fruit in terms of institutionalization? Low-cost actions?

Vinod Paul: Yes, here is one that is very low cost—this is something we don't see many funds doing: Large hedge funds do business continuity planning. Lots of new hedge funds are asked about disaster recovery, but many hedge funds ignore this. You have someone go in and look at processes going on within the firm: Who is doing what, how does your team work together from different locations, how will you operate? This is a very low-cost solution, and many firms should be doing this. This only costs a few hundred dollars to implement and have in place each month. The large funds understand the importance of business continuity planning as it ties to disaster recovery. Most funds should be doing this.

Richard Wilson: Great piece of advice. That sounds like one more puzzle
piece that hedge fund managers can clue into within this book in terms of
figuring out the 20 to 30 things they are not doing but could be to become
a more institutional-quality organization.

You work with so many diverse clients—this may be challenging, but
what is the most common bottleneck for further growth of individual
hedge funds?

Vinod Paul: The biggest challenge is that nobody wants to be the first one in.
Every investor wants to go in with others. One person had five investors
come in at one time so that nobody was the first group to put their toe in
the water. I thought that was a unique approach that I don't see very often.

Richard Wilson: What do you see in terms of growing a track record before
marketing a hedge fund? Are professionals building up three- to four-year
track records first, or marketing their funds right out of the gates with
perhaps immature operations in place?

Vinod Paul: A track record is of huge importance. Most small funds are
now starting much smaller than they wanted to. Lots of them are working
within the fund, trading for six months or a year before dedicating a full
team to raising capital, because investors sometimes like to see people who
can be successful on their own. They want to know the business is sound
and not based on raising a large amount of short-term money. I think the
money and talent are both out there but people are being very cautious,
wanting at least six months of proof. The investor wants to make sure the
manager has something at stake as well in the hedge fund business.

Richard Wilson: Have you seen any uptick in action within the hedge fund
start-up space? Our team has seen dozens of managers moving from investment banks and trading roles into launching their own hedge fund
business.

Vinod Paul: Yes, in the past three months, tremendous uptick in individuals
starting a hedge fund. Many professionals are leaving large organizations
and are making investments and taking that risk now. A lot of individuals
are taking this risk.

Richard Wilson: What would you suggest are the top three types of tools
that are most powerful or useful for hedge fund managers to use in their
business?

Vinod: Most hedge fund managers are not educated on the full array of
tools available to them today. If they need something, chances are the
tools are out there and they are affordable. A few years ago infrastructure
used to cost $200,000 when investors wanted sound disaster recovery,
compliance, and infrastructure on a very high level. For example, we have
an enterprise-level infrastructure. We can split that up and offer even just
two to three people a technology platform that has compliance, disaster

recovery, and business continuity all tied in. This is common now, to have the tools of a 1,000-person shop but only spend hundreds per user per month, not $200,000 on day one. This is now available from many vendors throughout the industry, and hedge fund managers should take advantage of this as they grow in order to get more done with fewer dollars. The top three tools I would suggest relate to:

1. Sound infrastructure setup—real corporate e-mail, real BlackBerry technology, file services, remote archiving, and so on.
2. Disaster recovery, so you can transfer with ease to another location in case of something happening.
3. Compliance—covering e-mail, infrastructure management (IM), policies, procedures, tools in place to ensure you are compliant with all regulations.

Richard Wilson: What trends do you see within the $1 billion-plus hedge fund space? What are they investing in?

Vinod Paul: Due to the size of their business they do not need every tool for risk management from an outside vendor, but they are looking at the best tools and being smart about their investments. They have larger teams so they have more educated professionals, or they engage consultants to help them find the better tools out there. A lot of these funds are being smarter about what they are doing because they have most expertise in-house and more choices in the marketplace.

Richard Wilson: Any last pieces of advice for hedge fund managers or professionals in the industry?

Vinod Paul: I deal with a lot of start-ups and professionals who are starting a hedge fund. I think the most successful guys are those who educate themselves. They take the time to really check out what options are out there right now, and don't rely on rumors of how much things cost. There is so much competition within the information technology (IT) space, and this is a huge benefit to hedge fund managers who now can pay much less than they may have just five to seven years ago. Every manager should educate themselves, differentiate themselves in how their processes are run and infrastructure is built.

NAKUL NAYYAR, QUANTITATIVE TRADING/SUPPORT, QUAD CAPITAL

Also for this chapter and for Chapter 5 on starting a hedge fund, I interviewed Nakul Nayyar from a U.S.-based hedge fund manager. He shared his experience on creating a more institutional-quality trading environment.

Richard Wilson: Could you please explain your professional background in hedge funds and trading in general? Please also include the story of how you got started in the industry, if you don't mind.

Nakul Nayyar: I graduated in 2002 from Johns Hopkins University into what was a difficult job environment. My first job out of school was actually in manufacturing, working as a project manager for a Fortune 500 company. After a few years of executing projects all over the Northeast, I began seriously contemplating a career change. I was actively managing my own accounts at the time and had some successful first attempts. With more luck than skill, I'm sure, at that time, I decided to leap first into trading. I quit my job, packed a suitcase, and moved to New York City. After a number of interviews—some quite unique, I should add—I landed a trading assistant role at a proprietary trading firm. My role was primarily to research and recommend growth/momentum stocks, using a mixture of event-driven fundamentals and technical analysis. Additionally, since I had an interest in derivatives, I managed the hedging of the overall portfolio.

Using that experience as a springboard, and after another set of very interesting interviews, I joined a small family office hedge fund with a focus on systematic and algorithmic-driven trading. Being a small fund, the firm had a start-up feel to it and an entrepreneurial spirit, meaning beyond the unglamorous daily tasks of keeping a fund running, I was allowed to research my own ideas and strategies and have these implemented. And while many strategies were automated, there were a few strategies that required manual execution or intervention. Additionally, as market conditions or regimes changed, it was important to refine, modify, or scrap existing strategies. The experience of creating a strategy through its life cycle (including sometimes its death) was extremely valuable and shaped my philosophy on trading immensely.

Richard Wilson: Thanks for sharing. It is interesting that you worked in the family office environment. I think that the experience of working in a family office is very valuable and often underestimated. I see such a demand for professionals wanting to work in hedge funds after graduation or some investment banking experience, but hardly anyone asks about getting into the family office industry.

How can a hedge fund manager improve the institutional feel and efficiency of his trading environment? Do you have a few methods or examples of how this can be accomplished?

Nakul Nayyar: A professional web site with password access is relatively inexpensive and can be done quickly. For start-ups especially, a web site allows all interested parties to quickly find your firm online and provides a perception of professionalism. Try to provide real content on the site and not some generic marketing talk to get interest. Spend some time on the bios as well; people are generally most interested in the background of the managers.

Additionally, there are all kinds of software that can be incorporated into your existing systems to crunch various statistics, generate reports, and do a number of other very useful functions without a lot of additional work. Talk to your brokers, prime brokers, and so on, and see what tools they may have available for free to assist your business. Or, alternatively, hiring programmers has become cheaper and cheaper.

Hire or learn quantitative measures and testing techniques even if the strategy is completely discretionary. Not only can it yield positive results for your trading, but it can be incorporated into your marketing documents as well. Data-driven research and reporting, in my opinion, is being valued much more highly than a keen eye or nicely annotated charts.

Richard Wilson: That is great advice—so many nuggets there I'm afraid that some may be missed. I agree that a professional web site is important, and I think that providing genuinely valuable content is even more effective. It helps build a relationship and position your fund principles or traders as experts and authorities in the space. This goes a long way with investors who want to make sure they are working with professionals who are not green to the business. Also, if anyone out there is looking to hire programmers, I have successfully hired and managed part-time contract programmers through a web site called Elance.com. It is a great resource that I have just started using for our firm.

Many other experts whom I interview in this book refer to carefully selecting the right service providers. I think that if you select them appropriately, you will have a leg up on competition due to the pedigree large service providers can lend you and the tools and reporting services they can also provide. This is especially true while choosing a fund administration firm and prime broker. Dig into checklists of exactly what they can provide, and make sure they actually follow through once everything is said and done.

HENDRIK KLEIN, CEO, DA VINCI INVEST LTD.

Our next interview related to fund operations and institutionalization is with Hendrik Klein, CEO of Da Vinci Invest Ltd., a Zurich-based hedge fund professional.

Richard Wilson: Hendrik, could you share a bit on your background and fund so we know the perspective from which you are answering these questions?

Hendrik Klein: I am CEO and founder of Da Vinci Invest. My specialization is relative value/volatility arbitrage, but we dare to think out of the box. So our strategy could be described as global macro (I look at the global markets with a macro-like approach) or commodity trading adviser (CTA). This is because we trade listed options and futures mainly. Our current fund size is $45 million, but we managed already over $300 million in total in this strategy.

Richard Wilson: Great, it is good to have some insights here from a European-based hedge fund manager running this type of a strategy. What operational resources does your firm leverage or use to help outsource work or improve the efficiency of the work your fund faces to keep business moving forward each month?

Hendrik Klein: Da Vinci Invest is domiciled in a so-called *hedge fund hotel*.

Richard Wilson: Hedge fund hotels have a mixed reputation here in the United States, and I know some managers are interested in just figuring out what services they provide to emerging fund managers. What services does the hedge fund hotel provide for you right now?

Hendrik Klein: They provide us with bookkeeping, tax advice, and IT maintenance. Software development is outsourced to IFIT and other outside companies.

Richard Wilson: How important do you see service providers being to the success of your fund? What process have you used to select these service providers, and what lessons have you learned about working with both the large and small service providers that your firm has worked with?

Hendrik Klein: We underestimated the service providers' part in the past. It is very important to have a good administrator, who delivers net asset value (NAV) in time and accurately. Additional services like sales fee calculation would be perfect. In the beginning we had an administrator who delivered NAV six to eight weeks too late. Our auditors never managed to finish the audit in the first or second quarter.

Richard Wilson: That certainly doesn't make things any easier while trying to grow your business. What was the result of that lack of service?

Hendrik Klein: One family office did not invest because of that. We lost a lot of reputation or credibility because of that.

Richard Wilson: That is a good case study, a story that will help managers pay attention and not underestimate the power of having solid service provider relationships and processes in place. So many times I stress the importance of working with solid service providers, but sometimes it takes a story like this to drive the point home.

　　What is the critical issue that decides whether you work with a particular consultant, service provider, or marketer? What is the one thing that you always look for? Good service? Recommendations from others? Branding? Experience?

Hendrik Klein: He should have time for us. That is, not having too many clients at the same time. The marketing should be done in good and in bad times.

Richard Wilson: What are the top three resources or tools that you use to run your hedge fund that are worth more than anything else? What are the most valuable resources that you could recommend to others?

Hendrik Klein: We use Bloomberg, Sol-3, and IFIT risk software with stress test scenarios. We can recommend all of these to hedge fund managers. In marketing we use Salesforce, but we are thinking about switching to Emnis soon.

Richard Wilson. I have come to find that Salesforce is the leading CRM system for fund managers—it helped me raise capital as well. What is the most challenging aspect of week-to-week or month-to-month operations? How has your firm adapted to this challenge? What tools have you found that help you manage this?

Hendrik Klein: Positive performance every month end. A strict risk management helps.

Richard Wilson: Do you have any other pieces of advice related to operational hedge fund best practices that you could share with other managers in the industry?

Hendrik Klein: Separate operational power between portfolio management and risk management.

Richard Wilson: What are your top five tips for hedge fund managers who have less than $100 million in assets under management but would like to improve the institutional quality of their fund?

Hendrik Klein: I actually have several suggestions for hedge fund managers who want to increase their institutional operations and trading:

- Launch a UCITS III fund, if possible with your strategy.
- List your fund on a stock exchange.
- Select the *best* service providers.
- Get due diligence reports.
- Get awards.

Richard Wilson: Great, thank you for that advice. What have you learned not to do, or what have you stopped doing related to trading or operations that was hurting your firm's position as a high-quality fund management business? Any lessons or tips to share on this point?

Hendrik Klein: I would have to say not selling straddles. We do not take unlimited risks anymore.

Richard Wilson: Besides AUM, what do you believe is most important for a hedge fund to focus on improving when thinking about institutionalizing a hedge fund? Risk management? Trading processes? Research? Pedigree?

Hendrik Klein: I believe that transparency, risk management, and clarity of investment process are the most important things. Anything you can do to upgrade the pedigree of the team helps.

 BONUS VIDEO MODULE

To watch a video on institutionalization and the importance of transparency for hedge fund managers, please type this URL into your Web browser: http://HedgeFundTraining.com/Transparency

---

Richard Wilson: I completely agree. One of the top three reasons this book was put together is that I believe hedge fund managers would like to hear from others on what has helped raise capital, make them more institutional, and improve operations. I think that some hedge fund managers or traders can feel somewhat alone in the industry and in their plans or challenges. Yet nowadays almost everyone I speak with is trying to upgrade their team pedigree and the caliber of their operations. This is one of the most widespread trends in the industry right now—the institutionalization of trading, risk management, marketing, team pedigree, and investment processes regardless of assets under management.

SHERI KANESAKA, ASSOCIATE, MICHELMAN & ROBINSON, LLP

The next interview on institutionalization was with Sheri Kanesaka of Michelman & Robinson, LLP, a law firm serving hedge fund managers and alternative investment professionals. She regularly handles complex, cross-border transactions and counsels on regulatory issues and compliance with U.S. securities laws and regulations for both private and public offerings.

Richard Wilson: In terms of making a hedge fund more institutional, what operational changes are you seeing being made?

Sheri Kanesaka: Probably one of the biggest trends right now, prompted in large part by the Madoff scandal and Ponzi schemes, is to have an external party do the fund administration such as the month-end investor reports/letters, analysis on positions, and so on. Prior to this trend, most of the hedge funds internally did the fund administration and provided the month-end reports. Now, however, investors want a third party to provide some oversight by reporting on the funds' books and records to make sure that investor monies are being invested in securities, derivatives, and so on. Most common is a monthly analysis and report.

Richard Wilson: I have seen the same trend. I have even spoken to board members of hedge funds who are now requiring their funds to use external administration firms or they will withdraw their board membership. I don't see this trend slowing down anytime soon.

Your firm works with many large hedge fund managers and asset management clients. Where do you see many of these firms investing their money back into? What could smaller funds learn from this?

Sheri Kanesaka: It is harder in this downturn (2008–2009) to access talent on all levels; harder to find them and retain them as management fees decline. Funds have to be creative in attracting, retaining, and compensating talent in this more challenging environment.

ERIC WARSHAL, CEO, FUND ASSOCIATES

The next interview was completed with Eric Warshal, CEO of Fund Associates, a fund administration firm based in Atlanta, Georgia. Mr. Warshal is a seasoned executive manager with over 15 years of operational management experience. Mr. Warshal spent 12 years with Cox Enterprises (a Fortune 200 company). He held various management positions in the company, ending his tenure as the director of operational support. Over the years he held positions of increasing responsibility that included product management, business development, research and development, technology management, and general operational management and support. His last position entailed managing the technology support of the 35,000 employees of Manheim Auctions (a Cox subsidiary). Mr. Warshal holds a bachelor of science in marketing from the University of Florida and a master of business administration from Emory's Goizueta Business School.

Richard Wilson: What operational best practices do you now see hedge funds picking up that are a new trend in the industry?

Eric Warshal: Although not entirely a new best practice, as a result of the scandals that have permeated the news recently, we have noticed an increase in the demand for cash management services that entail the administrator acting as a signatory for wire transfers on behalf of the fund.

This is directly reflective of the need to provide current and prospective investors with a level of confidence that the proper checks and balances are in place which prevent the opportunity for fraudulent activities to occur. Overall, we have identified more previously self-administered funds engaging in the best practice of hiring administrators to provide their investors and prospective investors with the confidence that an objective third party is validating their returns.

Richard Wilson: I'm glad you brought up the wire transfer and validation of returns points, because despite the common recommendation for hedge fund managers to obtain administration firm services, the direct reasons or benefits of doing so are sometimes not stressed enough. Anything else you see, any trends related to this advice?

Eric Warshal: We don't recommend particular investments; however, we are able to identify trends that occur in the trading of our clients. We notice that funds that properly utilize leverage seem to grow quicker than those that don't. However, it seems to be quite essential that, irrespective of what trading strategy they are implementing, they incorporate a hedge so as to offset their risk. We've seen funds that have grown quickly, by taking a large amount of risk, and we've seen them fall just as quickly.

Richard Wilson: I have seen similar things happen to very risky portfolios. I've worked closely on the third-party marketing and capital introduction/prime brokerage side of the business, and I often see both types of firms deny clients service if they are betting more than they are investing. Nobody wants to be associated with a manager aiming at 30 percent a month returns.

Everyone talks about the importance of operations, but from your perspective where should hedge fund managers be reinvesting their money to improve their operations?

Eric Warshal: Fund managers are realizing that there are both operational efficiencies and cost efficiencies associated with analyzing which operations can and should be accommodated for in-house and which should be outsourced. Fund managers can take advantage of consulting firms who can fully assess the manager's operational business and provide quantifiable justification for potential outsourcing of certain operations, such as technology, back-end office management, administration, and so on. Additionally there exists the added benefit of potentially becoming more appealing to institutional investors by virtue of properly outsourcing certain operations—to provide them with the level of comfort, knowing that certain operations are being handled by experienced professionals.

Richard Wilson: I think that documenting each key process your firm undertakes and making sure you have solid reasons for keeping each individual process in-house is an exercise every fund should walk through. What operational best practices do you see $1 billion-plus hedge funds implementing that almost all small hedge funds ignore or discount?

Eric Warshal: Proper due diligence is something that most small hedge funds tend to bypass, be it because of cost or just the fact that the fund doesn't have the overall time/resources to devote to it. However, the $1 billion-plus hedge funds take their time when deciding where and when to invest, with respect to other fund managers. By engaging in proper due diligence—that is, assessing the manager, his background, his past performance, his operations, and so on—they are able to more confidently invest and decrease their risk factors. However, smaller, less resource-intensive funds that solely rely upon the experience and intuition of their managers oftentimes only provide cursory levels of due diligence when making some fund investment decisions.

Richard Wilson: This is a topic that I touch on in detail in Chapter 6. I interview a family office, an institutional consultant, and provide some tips to managers who are moving through due diligence processes. I believe most professionals now recognize the importance of due diligence, but allocating the capital and finding the time will always be the bottleneck in the industry to actually implementing these best practices.

LANCE BARAKER AND WILLIAM KATTS, SENIOR MANAGING DIRECTORS, TRADESTATION PRIME

The final short interview for this chapter on institutionalization and operations improvement was with Lance Baraker and William Katts. As senior managing directors at TradeStation Prime, they meet and work with more than 500 hedge fund managers each year. Their experience is in working with $300 million to $1 billion-plus hedge funds as well as emerging hedge fund managers and start-ups.

Richard Wilson: What operational best practices do you now see hedge funds picking up that are a new trend in the industry?

Lance Baraker: There are several areas that a hedge fund needs to set up for operational best practices.

- Since the debacle of 2008 in the financial industry, risk management has come to the forefront of operational best practices. Hedge fund managers cannot access risk in a T+1 format any more.
- Managers need to understand the risk profile of their fund and determine the leverage, liquidity, and market risk. Managers should be offering

their institutional investors risk reports on demand and set up at least a weekly report going through the key risk metrics.

- Hedge fund managers should also segregate the duties of risk out to more than one person in their firm. That way the person picking the stocks is not the one determining the risk of the fund.
- Other key areas in operational best practices include valuation, compliance, disclosure, and business structure.

William Katts: I agree, but I would also like to stress that hedge funds must have the ability to consolidate multiple asset classes, multiple currencies, and multiple prime brokers in a single integrated platform in real time. Portfolio managers must, with a click of the mouse, be able to know exactly what their real time profit and loss (P&L), risk, and positions are. This trend is also to have a real-time reporting system that can be accessed by investors or a third party, moving toward a fully transparent model. The key trend in this market is full transparency.

Richard Wilson: Great advice. Out of the points you mentioned, I believe the segregation of risk and portfolio management duties is probably the least common suggestion I have seen actually implemented. This is something that I believe many $30 million-plus hedge funds could achieve but haven't yet.

Everyone talks about the importance of operations, but from your perspective, where should hedge fund managers be reinvesting their money to improve their operations?

Lance Baraker: Since the Bernie Madoff debacle, transparency is the buzzword going around the hedge fund industry. Hedge fund managers need capital to sustain their business, and this capital comes from institutional investors.

- The hedge fund managers who understand their demands will be the most successful.
- Right now daily or weekly transparency is essential.
- I would reinvest capital in technology that could produce daily reports.
- In addition, I would either hire a compliance officer or outsource this service to groups in the industry. Managers must have a written compliance manual and have a clear process in place for handling conflicts of interest in the hedge fund.
- I would also suggest the manager do a monthly call with investors to discuss the performance of the fund and thoughts on the strategy.
- Qualitative discussions are just as important as the quantitative reports.

Richard Wilson: I and several of the hedge fund managers and consultants I have interviewed strongly agree. You really need to understand your end client, their concerns, needs, wishes, and constraints, to operate in a way which is congruent with who they would like to invest in.

If you are a hedge fund manager or trader looking to start a fund, I would take some notes down on the bullet points listed by Lance Baraker and start creating a to-do list for your fund. Start with what can be implemented this week and make sure that it is done in a way that ensures the new processes or controls will be carried out consistently each week or month.

Richard Wilson: What best practices do you see $1 billion-plus hedge funds implementing that almost all small hedge funds ignore or discount?

Lance Baraker: I don't think smaller hedge funds are ignoring any best practices. However, I think the larger hedge funds have the capital to spend on compliance officers, risk managers, and technology. Most of the smaller hedge funds are usually one- or two-man shops that wear many hats and have money from family and friends. I think the service provider industry for hedge funds has grown, and you can outsource a tremendous amount of this to experts in their field. You can outsource compliance, disaster recovery, IT, valuation reporting, and middle- and back-office functions. This would save the smaller hedge fund time and money and still fulfill the best practices methodology it needs to be successful.

 BONUS VIDEO MODULE

To watch a video on institutional quality improvement opportunities for hedge funds, please type this URL into your Web browser: http://HedgeFundTraining.com/Institutional

Richard Wilson: True. Larger hedge funds can have 10 or 100 times the budget of an emerging hedge fund manager. I think outsourcing your noncore activities is the right way to go. I recently spoke with a fund manager in Boston at one of our Hedge Fund Premium networking events about this issue, and he mentioned that they had identified 18 core processes being carried out to run their fund. They have decided to outsource 15 of these. Most funds I know don't document every process they are carrying out and do not cleanly outsource them in this type of a strategic fashion. If you do it right it could have a few layers worth of benefits to investors who may be interested in examining your operations and what you do or do not keep in-house.

BONUS VIDEO MODULE

To watch a video on documenting operational hedge fund processes, please type this URL into your Web browser: http://
HedgeFundTraining.com/Operational

William, you have seen hundreds of hedge funds a year now and have
also been a trader for over 20 years. How do you see larger funds operating
in more institutional quality structures and how can small to medium-size
funds benefit from your perspective?

William Katts: Like Lance, I believe that it is not so much that smaller funds
are not aware of what best practices they should be employing. It just
comes down to economics and the amount of actual business they have
to spread to the street.

Two points that do really leap out, though, are (1) the ability to integrate
transparent real-time risk systems and reporting, and (2) the implementation of true multi-prime functionality. The price to incorporate the risk
systems and reporting can be quite costly versus the expected returns of
these smaller funds, and to multi-prime gives the larger funds the ability
to move assets between primes and extract more favorable fees than the
smaller funds. This also gives the allocators that feeling of safety across
custodians. We are growing our current business on the fact that many
small to medium-size hedge funds just haven't historically had the amount
of business to support these two abilities, yet many managers know that
they are critical to raising capital.

Richard Wilson: What should very quickly growing hedge funds of $100 mil-
lion invest their money in as they grow? What is most important?

William Katts: This may be oversimplified, but what is most important to a
hedge fund as they grow is investing in talent. This is extremely important
when implementing systems. Good systems are only as good as the ability
for them to be functional. The biggest complaint I hear from the bigger
hedge funds is that they are overstaffed with people who perform the same
job. Redundancy can escalate expenses. Also, the proper use of derivatives
can increase alpha and decrease risk. Having an experienced derivatives
trader is paramount—their ability to generate alpha and help a fund
manage risk is one of the key additions when the resources are available.
With the attrition of the trading floors and the advanced technology in
risk systems, the price for a talented person with proper risk tools becomes

much more cost-effective and an absolute must as a fund walks up the ladder.

Richard Wilson: Great, thank you both for sharing your insights. Few professionals that we interview here work closely with so many different hedge funds in the industry.

CHAPTER SUMMARY

Within this chapter we heard from many professionals who collectively have well over 100 years of experience within the industry. Here are some quick tips directly from their transcripts:

- Take the long-term view when planning out infrastructure and operations.
- Understand your USP; do SWOT analyses (strengths, weaknesses, opportunities, and threats); have superior sales literature and a web site in place.
- Invest in talent and possibly a derivatives trader with risk management experience.
- Most funds are considered institutional when they have over $80 or $100 million in AUM.
- Leverage service providers to gain access to additional real-time reporting, software, and risk management tools.
- Don't underestimate service providers—they are business partners who can make or break your business.
- Create transparent processes, risk monitoring, compliance procedures, and due diligence reports.

REVIEW QUESTIONS

1. True or false: A study by Capco in 2006 shows that more hedge funds fail due to poor performance and portfolio blow-up than for operational reasons.
2. Which of the following is not a piece of advice from Stephen Abrahams on improving hedge fund operations and capital-raising processes?
   a. Understand your strengths, weaknesses, and USP.
   b. Have better than average marketing materials and sales literature.
   c. Employ a third-party marketer or in-house sales professional.
   d. Fire your service providers and bring all of your operational work in-house to make sure everything is done the right way.

3. What AUM levels are typically considered the beginning of what a mature or institutional-quality firm would manage?
   a. Over $25 million AUM.
   b. Over $80 or $100 million AUM.
   c. Over $250 million AUM.
   d. Over $300 million AUM.
4. Hendrik Klein from Da Vinci Invest operates inside a hedge fund hotel. Which services do hedge fund hotels typically provide?
   a. Bookkeeping, tax advice, office space, IT maintenance.
   b. Bookkeeping, tax advice, capital raising, portfolio managers.
   c. Bookkeeping, portfolio management software, office space, IT maintenance.
   d. Bookkeeping, tax advice, capital raising, IT maintenance.
5. True or false: Working with the wrong service provider can result in lost investors for a hedge fund.
6. True or false: Within this chapter we suggest keeping risk and portfolio management together, as separating the operational powers of these departments may lead to many problems for a hedge fund business.
7. Since the Madoff case it has become _____ popular for hedge funds to use independent fund administration firms.
   a. Less.
   b. More.
8. Lance Baraker suggests that monitoring risk within a T+1 format is:
   a. Now a best practice and should be available to all hedge fund managers.
   b. Now the industry standard and just now becoming available.
   c. Not adequate anymore.
9. Within this chapter it is suggested that _____ or _____ transparency helps ease investor concerns.
   a. Monthly or annual.
   b. Weekly or monthly.
   c. Daily or weekly.
   d. Weekly or quarterly.
10. True or false: William Katts suggests that talent is an overrated resource that small hedge funds spend too much money on.

   Answers: To view the answers to these questions, please see http://HedgeFundTraining.com/Answers.

CHAPTER 3

Hedge Fund Marketing Pro

There are three ways to raise capital: having more high net worth friends than the next fund manager, landing early institutional allocations, or hard work. Get to work.

This chapter provides some basic capital raising and marketing tips, as well as a case study analysis of Tassini Capital Management, a California-based hedge fund manager. Tassini Capital Management was attempting to grow its assets from $39.2 million in assets under management (AUM) to $250 million in AUM in a three-year period. The case study outlines the management's struggles, challenges, lessons learned, and the formula they found for raising capital from new investors. This chapter provides some short interviews on capital raising, as well.

Why important: The capital-raising tips, strategies, and case study included in this chapter are only available due to lessons learned the hard way, through making mistakes, receiving feedback, and adjusting capital-raising strategies until they worked. Studying this chapter carefully can save literally $25,000 or more in consulting fees and, more importantly, double the rate at which you raise capital. If these lessons and tips are ignored, your team will likely repeat mistakes that others often make while trying to grow their AUM.

 BONUS VIDEO MODULE

To watch a video on hedge fund marketing, please type this URL into your Web browser: http://HedgeFundTraining.com/Marketing

BAD NEWS

The bad news is there is no magic bullet to raising capital. I spoke with at least a dozen managers recently at a Hedge Fund Premium networking event in Chicago regarding their capital-raising plans. Most were looking for capital-raising help of some type, and we discussed many roadblocks that managers are seeing between them and the AUM levels they are trying to achieve.

Daily action and discipline are the best things that fund managers can do to raise capital. They must take responsibility for marketing their fund and have someone reaching out to new investors on a daily basis. If they do not, they will forever remain in the bottom 20 percent of the industry in terms of assets. Very few funds gain their initial assets through a superpowerful third-party marketing firms. Third-party marketers typically like to work with managers who have some AUM momentum or foundation underneath them.

To raise capital, managers need to have superior tools and processes to those of their competitors. This means superior investor cultivation processes in place, superior investor relationships management, superior marketing materials, superior outreach efforts, superior e-mail marketing, and superior focus on investors who actually have the potential of making an investment. Each of those topics could be discussed for a whole conference, and all of these moving parts need to be in place to compete in today's industry. While this does not mean that managers need to outspend others in marketing, they do need to strategically plan their marketing campaigns to compete effectively.

There is a good quote which goes something like, "If you want to have what others don't, you have to do what others won't." In other words, translated for hedge fund marketing: If you want to grow assets, you must put in the extra work, planning, and strategy that others skip over.

Every morning, try to listen to a 45-minute custom MP3 audio session of business lessons, marketing tips, and positive thinking notes. One great quote I hear every morning is connected to an interview Brian Tracy conducts in which a multimillionaire says that success is easy: "You must decide exactly what it is you want, and then pay the price to get to that point." All of this may sound wishy-washy or inexact, but it is important to realize that there is no single magic bullet for raising capital. It takes hard work, trial, and a superior effort on all fronts to stand out from your competition.

BONUS VIDEO MODULE

To watch a video on third-party marketing please type this URL into your Web browser: http://HedgeFundTraining.com/3PM

PUBLIC RELATIONS MANAGEMENT

Public relations has to be one of the most ignored marketing tools of hedge fund managers today. The Hedge Fund Group has worked with over three dozen hedge funds on their marketing plans and capital-raising efforts. So far, the most intense public relations effort our firm has seen set forth by a sub–$1 billion hedge fund was a single press release over a four-year period. This is not to say that any hedge fund that is not publishing at least four press releases per year is doing something wrong. However, many could benefit by simply making themselves more available to the press.

The media is hungry for real-time opinions of hedge fund managers, traders, and marketers. They need comments on current market conditions, trends in hiring and firing of traders and portfolio managers, and what prospects lie ahead for the industry as a whole.

Many hedge fund managers shy away from contributing to stories in the press. I would strongly encourage you to speak with your legal counsel and see if they would approve of your discussions with the media if you stick to industry trends, general market trends, and long-term movements you are seeing in the industry.

Top Four Tips for Taking Advantage of Public Relations for Your Hedge Fund

1. Speak to your legal counsel to check on exactly what you can or cannot say to the press.
2. Develop a list of 10 to 15 targeted publications that you would like to appear in. Identify the editors of financial columns in those publications or news sources and introduce yourself to them as a resource.
3. Speak at public events, conferences, networking events, and other places in the industry where you will be heard not only by others in the industry but probably by a few members of the press as well.
4. Consider writing a book on your insights and experience. Many professionals in the hedge fund industry are often interviewed on TV after they

have published a book on a specific topic in the hedge fund industry, such as regulation or quantitative trading. Yes, writing a book sounds extreme to many who are already working 50 hours a week, but that is also why it would be so effective to consider doing so. Those with the time and skills to write well are often not the same ones who have the experience and insight to write something unique and valuable.

 BONUS VIDEO MODULE

To watch a video on public relations strategies for hedge funds, please type this URL into your Web browser: http://HedgeFundTraining .com/PR

EDUCATIONAL MARKETING

One of the most effective ways you can market your hedge fund is by being four times more educational and easy to understand than your competition. I wrote in my blog last year that a recent survey had shown that over 78 percent of institutional investors will not invest in something that they cannot understand. I would imagine that for high net worth (HNW) investors this figure is even higher.

While some managers purposely position their fund to appear "black box" and top secret, there are opportunities to market hedge funds which are open, transparent, and simple in explaining the fund's investment process and risk management tools. This does not mean ignoring advanced methods or models of trading and managing portfolios, but it would require more of a 10,000-foot-view and explanation of the investment process instead of the 500-foot-views that are so often used. The trick in doing this right is to balance providing enough detail and real meat that an institutional investor or consultant will gain some granularity, while not completely overwhelming HNW investors or wealth managers who may be less versed in common hedge fund strategies of portfolio management techniques.

Here is a list of four additional ways you may market your hedge fund in a more educational or simple way:

1. *PowerPoint.* Dedicate 20 percent of the PowerPoint presentation to educational content. Asterisk all industry terms and note that definitions are provided in the back of the presentation. Explain the investment

process so that anyone could understand, at least on a high level, how your fund operates. Start with the team, high-level investment process, and how that all comes together before digging into trading examples or risk management tools.

2. *Folder.* Many managers use a folder of marketing materials while meeting with clients. This often includes a one pager, a PowerPoint presentation, and a recent quarterly market outlook newsletter written by the portfolio manager. It is wise to always include some additional reading in the folder as well. Provide two to three white papers written by experts outside of the firm that speak to the trends related to the assets that your firm invests in or strategies your firm employs.

3. *Speaking and writing.* Speaking at wealth management conferences and HNW-related events can be highly effective. The easily overlooked aspect here is audience: Are there more competitors or potential investors at the events you speak at?

4. *Wealth management and financial planners.* Some of the most ignored sources of capital for hedge fund managers are small to medium-size wealth management firms and financial planning groups that serve HNW professionals from time to time but don't manage $1 billion-plus in total assets. Many of these groups work as part of a broker-dealer network or RIA, and they may only meet in person with 5 to 10 hedge funds in any one year, whereas larger institutions may meet with several each week. These relationships take a long time to build into effective sources of capital, but if they are approached in a more educational fashion than your institutional leads, they can pay off as very sticky long-term accounts.

 BONUS VIDEO MODULE

To watch a video on educational marketing strategies for raising capital, please type this URL Into your Web browser: http://HedgeFundTraining.com/Educational

FORGET ABOUT CONTACTING MORE INVESTORS

Yes, it may seem illogical to forget about contacting new investors while attempting to raise capital, but this may be what you need to do to meet your business goals. Many of the hedge fund managers I speak to want to be connected with investors; they want lists of family offices, seed capital providers, or HNW wealth management firms. While accessing more investor contact details may be a useful resource and improve your marketing efforts, it is often not the real constraint that is holding your business back.

 BONUS VIDEO MODULE

To watch a video on called "What Is a Family Office?" please type this URL into your Web browser: http://HedgeFundTraining.com/Family-Office

No business is perfect; every business has some constraint that, if removed, would help the business more than anything else. Sometimes this constraint is portfolio management expertise, sometimes it is marketing materials, and many times it is lack of institutionalized processes and tools. Seldom do I meet with hedge funds which, if provided with a long list of 1,000 investors, would explode in assets under management.

Most hedge funds do not take the time to write down all of their current business problems or symptoms and ask four "why" questions to identify the root constraint in their business model. A good tool that I have seen used by half a dozen management consulting gurus is the "Four Why Process." If you ask why something is happening four times, you will often get to the root cause of the problem. Here's an example of how the process is used:

- *Initial problem/symptom*: We don't manage $100 million in assets yet. Why?
- *Potential answer and follow-up question*: We are not raising capital from wealth management firms as you had hoped. Why?
- *Potential answer and follow-up question*: Our marketing materials have not been brought up to speed with the competition's—they are light and our investment process is poorly described. Why?
- *Potential answer and follow-up question*: We know that you should be paying a consultant or in-house marketer to help with both marketing materials and generating relationships, but you have not hired one. Why?
- *Potential answer*: We do not have the profits available to hire a full-time marketer, but we can get around to creating a system to share equity, grow relationships with third-party marketers, or build a marketing-related advisory board.

The point of this exercise is to identify what the bottleneck is that is slowing down your growth. If a hedge fund can be seen as a 20-link chain, you must have all 20 strong links in place to keep the business growing long-term. If 19 links can carry the weight of a $300 million fund but one link is only up to par for a $10 million fund, then you will limit your growth and may never reach or only very slowly grow into a $300 million fund. The biggest return for your investment of time and money will be to focus on fixing that one broken or subpar link in your operations, marketing, trading, or internal business processes. Anything else would be a relative waste of money or energy.

This is a unique marketing technique because it is a reminder that the smartest thing you could do for your marketing and sales campaign may have nothing to do with picking up a phone or buying a database of investors. Before spending more money or valuable time, consider the following two tips for improving your ability to attract investors:

1. *Use the "Four Why Tool"* to drill down deeper into the top five problems that you see your fund facing right now. Oftentimes three to five problems will be symptoms of a single root cause which can be directly addressed.
2. *Ask others,* including your advisory board, current investors, potential investors and co-workers, what is holding your fund back. Do not settle with two-word surface answers. Try to identify what three to five action steps your fund could take this quarter to improve how you are positioned and address the number one limiting factor in your business.

 BONUS VIDEO MODULE

To watch a video called "What Is Holding Your Hedge Fund Back?" please type this URL into your Web browser: http://HedgeFundTraining.com/Holding

E-MAIL MARKETING BEST PRACTICES

I worked as a risk consultant and capital raiser for seven years before starting my own firm. During the last few years of those positions, I was responsible for raising most assets on an e-mail and phone-based system, and I have slowly picked up some tips for capital raising since then. Our business is so e-mail-based (800,000 messages in two years) that we have been forced to study best practices in this space to improve our efficiency at connecting with potential clients. Here are the e-mail marketing strategies we have picked up the hard way over the past few years.

Most CEOs don't invest their time or put much importance on managing e-mail communications. If you invest your time in increasing your effectiveness at e-mail marketing you will have an edge over others.

E-Mail Marketing Best Practices

1. *Understanding importance of copy.* What is the difference between a $1 bill and a $100 bill? The message on the paper. The message on your e-mail, the message on your investor letters, the message on everything you write makes the difference between its being worth $1,000 and $100,000. I think that sales copy writing is consistently undervalued and overlooked by business and investment professionals of all types. One of the best tips I can provide for e-mail marketing would be simply not to overlook the power of a carefully constructed e-mail marketing campaign or well-written piece of communication.

2. *Use the professional's first name in the subject of e-mails to them.* Marketing Sherpa 2008 study showed this practice increased open rates by 30 percent; using both the first and last name increased open rates by 22 percent.

3. *Focus on the headline.* The most important part of any piece of copy is the headline. Oftentimes over e-mail the headline of the e-mail is a slight variation of the subject line, perhaps the subject line minus the person's first name. Focus on fitting a benefit and then the chain reaction of that benefit into the headline if possible: "Double Your Capital Raising Resources to Cultivate More Investors Each Day." We have found that putting the benefit after your firm name is most effective. Just be careful not to promise benefits that are at odds with your compliance department or the core of what you are really offering.

4. *Focus on the start.* Hook the reader in the first paragraph. Make sure the first paragraph is no longer than two sentences and provides a very concise summary as to what will be discussed in the following message. If possible, try to fit in both what the benefits will be of hearing this information and what the dangers are of not paying attention to it. Psychological studies consistently show that professionals are almost twice as likely to listen more closely and take action on information related to a fear or some negative result than on some potential benefit or positive outcome. This does not mean you should scare clients into working with you, but you should hook readers by using *framing*, which

mentions the positive results as well as the negative consequences of not taking action. The recent use of e-mail browsers that let you preview the first 50 to 150 words of e-mail messages makes the start of your e-mail even more important.

5. *Use professional e-mail distribution services.* Use a professional e-mail distribution service such as AWeber. This costs $10/month or less to start using. By using this service your e-mails will be delivered more often, your campaigns will be more organized, and the service will more than pay for itself through saving you valuable time. Make sure that whatever service you use, you consider opt-in confirmation and enable an unsubscribe link at the bottom of each e-mail you send.

6. *Automate relationship development.* Use automated follow-up e-mails. Write a series of 20 educational e-mails covering industry white papers, industry findings, commonly misunderstood terms, and information about your fund. Once you have qualified an investor, ask for their permission to opt into an e-mail list which will automatically send them these professional papers once a month for the next 20 months. If you deliver value in each of these 20 e-mails, your further inquiries will be well received. We currently use Aweber to send out automated e-mails to over 50,000 professionals each month.

7. *Use stories.* Whenever you are writing an e-mail or sales letter, try to incorporate a story of some type. How was this product created? How did your career and experience evolve and bring you to this point where you have gained this knowledge? If you read the early part of this chapter you will see that I have a short story about my own experience with e-mail marketing which led me to write this chapter. This helps create a frame of reference for the reader and can be helpful in many cases.

8. *Include a picture and signature.* End your communication with a picture of the professional on the team who is held out as the communicator or leader. Make sure that a real scanned signature and professional picture are included to help readers connect with your team.

Our team provides over 1,600 hedge funds a year with capital-raising advice, resources, and products. Our team has helped raise hundreds of millions of dollars in capital as well. Through these two sources of experience we see many of the same fund marketing mistakes made over and over again. If you can avoid these mistakes, you will be more effective than 80 percent of your competitors in the marketplace.

Top 10 Fund Marketing Mistakes
1. You have a three-month capital raising goal. This is unrealistic and the wrong mind-set to go out of the gate with. You need to plan, build

relationships, educate potential clients, and design high-quality marketing strategies and materials for the long term. It takes time to raise lots of capital, and usually the more valuable the investor, the longer the sales cycle. Don't try to cram everything into a one- to three-month capital raise.

2. You're counting on simply building a track record and then hoping to outsource all marketing to a great third-party marketing firm down the road. This puts all of your eggs into the third-party marketing basket. Third-party marketers have hundreds of potential clients approaching them each year. It is risky to assume one will not only take you on as a client but actually raise a sustainable level of capital for you.

3. You're spending $8,000 on graphic design and web site design but $0 on hiring someone who is an expert at constructing sales letters, writing copy, and creating effective headlines and taglines for your positioning in the marketplace. Many times I see fund managers who want to look very professional but there is no meat in what they are saying, no hook to draw in the reader.

4. Not dedicating resources to capital raising is the most obvious mistake that I see in the industry. Many fund managers will act as the CIO, make two to three phone calls a week or sometimes per month, and then wonder why they have not raised more capital. Performance does *not* market itself, pedigree does *not* swing all doors wide open. You need to have dedicated resources, an internal marketing resource working at least 20 hours/week, investor databases so you can spend your time calling on real prospects instead of always having to qualify them, and a growing internal customer relationship management (CRM) or investor relationship management (IRM) system in place to track the results of your investment in investor relationships.

5. You speak at conferences full of your closest competitors instead of your highest-value potential investors.

6. You underestimate the value of a first-name-basis relationship with your top investor prospects. Some professionals, especially those with technical backgrounds, think that marketing is a numbers game. Yes, you sometimes have to reach out to many to develop relationships with few, but relationships are at the core of everything that gets done. Like Jeffrey Gitomer says, "All things equal, people like to do business with friends; all things being unequal, people still like to do business with friends."

7. Another mistake I see in the hedge fund space is a lack of capital-raising training or fund-marketing instruction. You do not have to pay to have your marketing staff trained, but at the very least you should document your own best practices, processes, and investor pipeline development

plans, so they can be easily communicated to team members and board members and then constantly improved each quarter.

8. You miss the boat on authority positioning, educational forms of marketing, and improving your own pedigree standing within the industry.
9. You write off PR. Most managers shy away from or completely ignore public relations as an avenue for helping create interest and positioning for experts on their team. Many funds have now successfully employed the media to spread messages about their fund.
10. A mistake that I see more than 90 percent of funds doing today is using a boring, run-of-the-mill unique selling proposition (USP) or, worse yet, not having one at all.

COPY WRITING

Copy writing is the use of words to promote a person, business, opinion, or idea.

Copy writing is the most undervalued and overlooked tool that a marketer or sales professional can develop. Many professionals value cold-calling skills, networking, branding, or public relations skills but I think that copy writing skills are the most valuable.

Top Five Reasons Copy Writing for Capital Raising Is Important
1. The headline of letters, subject line of e-mails, and first few words of speeches are the most important. Crafting a great headline can take hours to complete, but it will make the difference between being shown to others and never being noticed.
2. Many hedge funds, family offices, and private equity groups spend over $20,000 of their money on their marketing materials every year, yet 95 percent of decisions are based on what's always been done or what sounds good instead of A/B testing results to find what is effective.
3. Every investment fund markets itself using e-mails and investor letters. Without copy writing skills you may not only be failing to connect with your audience but you could actually be turning them off and pushing clients away.
4. Investment funds of all types are started by successful traders and portfolio managers; very few are started only by marketers. Due to this nature of how the business is founded and grown, managers overlook niche marketing practices such as copy writing or see them as something beneath them.
5. Ninety-nine percent of your competitors are not using copy writing best practices.

BONUS VIDEO MODULE

To watch a video on the importance of copy writing for capital raising, please type this URL into your Web browser: http://HedgeFundTraining.com/Copywriting

CASE PROFILE

Fund name	Tassini Capital Management
Strategy	Long/short
Track record	4 years and 8 months
AUM	$39.2 million
Team	Brian Tassini, co-portfolio manager
	Chris Tassini, co-portfolio manager
	John Travis, junior portfolio analyst
	Mary Powers, administrative assistant

In the past, Tassini Capital Management has conducted all marketing efforts in-house, using Chris Tassini's background in business and marketing to approach potential investors. Over a period of four years their fund grew from just $2 million at inception to $39.2 million. Their current AUM profile is made up of family and friends' money, high net worth accredited investors, and wealth management firms. Figure 3.1 is a diagram showing this breakdown in assets under management.

AUM in Millions

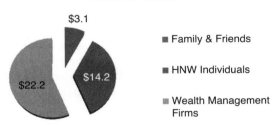

FIGURE 3.1   AUM Distribution in Millions, Tassini Capital Management

In the past, the team only spent a collective 15 hours a week in marketing the fund or promoting their brand in the industry. This was carried out by Chris Tassini, and most outgoing sales calls were to investors he had met at conferences or networking events in the industry.

Tassini Capital Management has recently hired a proven third-party marketing team to help them raise capital from new investors. A third-party marketer is a professional who independently raises capital for fund managers on a contractual basis, often raising capital for multiple funds at any given time (learn more at ThirdPartyMarketing.com). The goal is for Tassini Capital Management to raise a total of $210 million and bring total AUM up to $250 million in three years.

From the very first day of working together, the third-party marketing team started to make changes to the marketing materials, investor relationship management systems, investor databases, execution, and processes followed while raising capital. The first change made was to the marketing materials of the fund. Tassini Capital Management had a new logo developed, its PowerPoint presentation expanded, and one-pager redesigned as well. A one-pager is a concise overview of a hedge fund's track record, team, performance ratios, and relative performance. The most important changes were made to the PowerPoint presentation, often referred to as a *deck* or *pitch book* in the industry. The advice the third-party marketing firm gave to Tassini Capital Management regarding the pitch book included these tips:

- Make the competitive advantage clear—make sure that the hedge fund has a *unique* selling proposition (USP), not just a selling proposition. Most funds talk about diversification and a unique investment process or team without much meat or real unique advantage presented.
- There should be three main areas of focus in the PowerPoint presentation: team pedigree and experience, investment process, and risk controls.
- Work with the highest-quality service providers possible so that the fund does not get scrutinized more than it already will in the normal course of due diligence.
- Use prime brokerage and fund administration business partners to improve your marketing materials. These two service providers often provide reporting and risk management aspects which beef up the institutional feel of the organization.
- Do not ever let the marketing presentation be longer than 30 pages. It is challenging enough to get the attention of an investor long enough to thoroughly review a one-page marketing piece on your firm.
- Purchase premium graphics for $2 at iStockphoto.com; develop professional logos for your fund at Design99.com.

■ Update the PowerPoint presentation quarterly with current performance numbers that have been verified by the administrator or auditor.

BONUS VIDEO MODULE

To watch a video on unique selling propositions (USP), please type this URL into your Web browser: http://HedgeFundTraining.com/USP

Investor relationship management (IRM) systems were the next thing that the third-party marketing firm improved. In the past, Tassini Capital Management used a Microsoft Word investor tracking system, when one was used at all. Now they pay a small amount per month for an account with Salesforce.com, which allows them to track the history of their communications with each investor and, even more importantly, alerts the team when another contact point is needed with a potential investor. It took a few months for the Tassini Capital Management staff to figure out how to use everything in Salesforce.com, but ultimately they found it powerful and flexible to adjust as their fund grew.

BONUS VIDEO MODULE

To watch a video on investor relationship management (IRM) please type this URL into your Web browser: http://HedgeFundTraining.com/Investor-Relationship-Management

Investor databases are something that Tassini Capital Management had never used in the past. Through InvestorDatabases.com and with help from the third-party marketer, they obtained contact details for over 1,000 potential investors and put together a strategic plan for approaching 200 of them at any given time.

The method by which Tassini Capital Management was raising capital in the past was not effective. In addition to not using an IRM system, the team had somewhat randomly been approaching many different types of investors, from large European banks to small seed capital providers. The third-party marketing firm consulted Chris and Brian Tassini and found that they were both unwilling to part with equity ownership in the management company of the fund in exchange for capital. They also reviewed past notes and confirmed that all efforts to work through institutional investment consultants had been stalled due to sub–$100 million AUM levels. The result was a much more focused method of systematically approaching a mix of investors which included 10 percent institutional investment consultants, 50 percent wealth management firms, 20 percent multifamily offices, and 20 percent high net worth individuals. While institutional investment consultants were not going to invest any time soon, they were kept in the mix so that the team could continue to receive valuable institutional feedback from the consultants.

Despite having hired an experienced third-party marketing firm for assistance in raising capital, Tassini Capital Management consistently faced two main challenges while developing relationships with investors. The first challenge was catching the attention of a potential investor. With so many competitors in the industry offering similar strategies, it was hard to stand out from the crowd. Convincing a potential investor to engage in a 40-minute due diligence call was often in and of itself relatively significant. The second challenge the team faced was the noninstitutional feeling that potential investors got while looking at their sub–$40 million portfolio and team of four professionals. The business looked unsteady and unproven to larger institutional firms that typically had expectations of $80 to $150 million as a very minimum needed before allocations are made.

Over two years of trial and error and receiving advice from other managers, Tassini Capital Management adjusted its marketing approach in several ways to meet these challenges. Three changes included:

1. Implementing an institutional-quality multiple-modality marketing approach including e-mail marketing, conference speeches, article writing, phone calls, and traditional mailings. Each team member had a different role in this marketing approach which supplemented the work completed by the third-party marketer.
2. Developing prewritten and scripted responses to questions regarding the institutional quality of the firm's trading, technology, risk management, and investment research processes. This attention to these specific areas of operations led to consistent improvements in how they are carried out. Many of these changes were suggested by free-to-access institutional investment consultants who had been called upon for feedback.
3. Constructing a sense of authority status around the firm through its presence in the market. The team members matched this awareness in the industry with improved branding and marketing materials and tried to leverage this to meet in person with as many potential investors as possible. Meeting investors face-to-face allowed them to get past the gatekeeper at many wealth management and family office firms.

BONUS VIDEO MODULE

To watch a video on systematic capital-raising tips, please type this URL into your Web browser: http://HedgeFundTraining.com/ Systematic

STEPHEN ABRAHAMS, VICE PRESIDENT OF MARKETING FOR A LONDON-BASED HEDGE FUND

For this chapter's first interview, I sat down with Stephen Abrahams, who raises capital for a London-based boutique hedge fund manager. Here he shares some lessons and tips on what he has been doing to raise assets for his fund.

Richard Wilson: What tips could you provide to hedge fund capital raisers on developing investor relationships?

Stephen Abrahams: Keep in touch on a regular basis, find out what they are looking for, and ask for as much feedback as possible, good or bad. See if you can help them in any way, and always verify that you are speaking with the right person at the firm.

Richard Wilson: That is good advice. The rule of thumb that I used while raising capital was to keep in touch with my top prospects by mail, e-mail, or phone once every 10 days, or about every week and a half. With lower-priority prospects I would try to keep in touch twice a month in some way. Do you use a CRM system of some type to manage investor prospects?

Stephen Abrahams: We do not right now but I think they are a good idea.

Richard Wilson: I have used SalesForce and found it effective, but I have also used an Excel spreadsheet to simply track investor contact details. I know many professionals, though, simply use Outlook's contact databases, task manager, and reminder system. How do you track the development of your sales pipeline? Do you rate investor prospects to keep them in priority follow-up order?

Stephen Abrahams: I use an Excel sheet and contact cards along with Outlook tasks and calendar synched to my iPhone.

Richard Wilson: How many investors is your hedge fund approaching or calling in any three-month period—400 investors, 50 investors, 1,000 investors?

Stephen Abrahams: I approach 50 to 100 investors, but it would depend, as I prefer to research and target more likely prospects rather than use a shotgun approach to cultivating new investors.

PRATIK SHARMA, MANAGING DIRECTOR, ATYANT CAPITAL

For the next interview in this chapter I met with Pratik Sharma, managing director of Atyant Capital, who has launched and raised capital for several hedge funds in the past, learning some lessons and picking up ways of doing business right along the way.

Richard Wilson: Pratik, can you first share what some of your experience includes?

Pratik Sharma: I've launched two funds in the past four years. One is a long-only, deep-value fund focused on middle-market Indian equities. The second one is a precious metals focused L/S fund investing in equities, ETFs, futures, and options. I've had to learn foreign regulations from scratch, learn how to work effectively with offshore service providers, and do all the marketing and client relations work. I'm not a portfolio manager, I am a capital raiser with a background in sales and management consulting.

Richard Wilson: What types of marketing materials do you use to market your fund to new potential investors? Anything really unique?

Pratik Sharma: It's pretty standard. We use a standard pitch book/fact sheet. We are in the process of creating a more dynamic web site that integrates a blog, performance reports, and all of our social networking efforts.

Richard Wilson: Do you use a CRM system? How do you track important investor relationships or potential investor contact details?

Pratik Sharma: Yes, we use Salesforce.com to track our investor relationships and to keep track of important developments over the long term.

Richard Wilson: That's great. I have used Salesforce as well—it is a tool that, if used right, I think can really improve the long-term ability to raise capital even if it does take some extra time to store everything in the system up front. Does your firm build organic investor databases or purchase investor databases from others?

Pratik Sharma: We build our databases organically over time. Our web site is designed to drive inbound interest and to keep that interest.

Richard Wilson: Some investor databases are not organized for capital raising and can be a relative waste of time. How long is your typical investor sales cycle? Eight months? Twelve months? Eighteen months?

Pratik Sharma: We are focused on high net worth individuals and family offices. When we raise capital from high net worth individuals our sales cycle is two to three months.

Richard Wilson: What is the most valuable lesson you have learned while raising capital over the past few years?

Pratik Sharma: You *must* have an easy-to-explain and compelling unique selling proposition.

Richard Wilson: I am so glad you mentioned that, because I think it is underestimated. To an investor who sees 100 presentations a month, everyone looks the same, and it is hard to be truly unique and convey that effectively in a meaningful way. Is there any one book, resource, tactic, or tool that has noticeably increased the ability of your firm to reach new investors and raise more capital?

Pratik Sharma: We have found that white papers and webinars are the most useful tools. They serve as a source of knowledge and insight for your investors and help to grow the existing relationship. These tools build credibility and demonstrate value even before a formal relationships starts.

Richard Wilson: That is great. I know that this really works, and our firm uses educational materials such as our free e-book on hedge funds for this same reason. We provide something that benefits our potential clients, and then when they have a capital-raising or training-related need we can be ready for them when they need us. I think that your fund is ahead of 90 percent of the hedge funds I speak to in realizing that if they invest their time and energy into giving away educational content, free training, webinars, resources, and so on, it will come back to them several times over through greater total and more loyal investors.

What are your top five tips to hedge fund managers who have less than $100 million in assets under management but would like to improve the institutional quality of their fund?

Pratik Sharma: I would suggest investing in your web site. Try to get feedback from trusted contacts. Have a real USP that isn't just fluff—then you will attract more investors than others in the industry.

Richard Wilson: Besides AUM, what do you believe is most important for a hedge fund to focus on improving when thinking about institutionalizing a hedge fund? Risk management? Trading processes? Research? Pedigree?

Pratik Sharma: Risk management *is* trading. It is the way one really generates alpha. Also, internal risk management (governance, controls) is key.

Richard Wilson: Agreed. I think that strict, independent governance and controls are something that will be a must-have in five years instead of a nice-to-have, as they seemingly are right now.

Now that your hedge fund has grown a bit and has been around for a few years what do you wish you had known when you first started your hedge fund? What should every new hedge fund start-up know that you wish someone had told you?

Pratik Sharma: This business is the best in the world. It is still all about doing the best for your customers. The arrogance and nonalignment of interests in hedge funds has been atrocious over the last several years. Investors aren't stupid and they aren't going to put up with it anymore. Embrace that as a differentiator, but recognize that you have to *do* it and not just say it.

Richard Wilson: Great to hear that from a marketer. What three tips or pieces of valuable advice could you lend to emerging hedge fund managers or new hedge fund start-ups? What valuable lessons have you learned from starting your fund, trading in the fund, and growing it that others in similar situations could learn from?

Pratik Sharma: Get good service providers. Size is not necessarily better. Some good administrators focus on early stage managers. They can be a tremendous help.

Richard Wilson: I agree. While sometimes the brand or reputation of the service provider may be important, I do think that there are times when large service providers leave small hedge fund clients behind in terms of service.

How long did it take you to launch your fund? About how much did it cost in total, and what was the most difficult or time-consuming part about this process?

Pratik Sharma: We formed an offshore fund for India, which took three months. Regulatory approvals were the most time-consuming part. Onshore U.S. Limited Partnership (LP) took 30 days. The most difficult part is that the manager has to manage the various entities involved. It is a project, and if you don't stay on top of all the moving pieces, it will result in delays and increased expense.

Richard Wilson: Can you share a few mistakes or setbacks you encountered that were painful and didn't have to be experienced?

Pratik Sharma: Don't have a bad or nondescript USP. You will get laughed out of some offices.

Richard Wilson: Definitely worth repeating that point—I agree. What are the top three resources or tools that you use to run your hedge fund that are worth more than anything else? What are the most valuable resources that you could recommend to others?

Pratik Sharma: Salesforce.com and ConstantContact.com are probably two of the most useful tools.

Richard Wilson: What is the critical issue that determines whether you work with a particular consultant, service provider, or marketer? What is the one thing that you always look for? Good service? Recommendations from others? Branding? Experience?

Pratik Sharma: It is a bit hard to describe. The best way I can articulate it is "make sure there is a good fit" in terms of experience, in terms of expectations, and in terms of personalities. These service providers are extensions of your organization. You want to make sure that you feel comfortable having them interact with your clients. Your clients will call them.

Richard Wilson: Exactly. I think that in some businesses you may use a service provider to get Internet, or to find new talent for your team, and they are truly outside of your organization. In the hedge fund industry, though, you are really outsourcing large chunks of your operations and processes to these firms, so this is an important decision, whether it is a third-party marketing, prime brokerage, or fund administration firm.

What is the most challenging aspect of week-to-week or month-to-month operations? How has your firm adapted to this challenge? What tools have you found that help you manage this?

Pratik Sharma: The challenge is not to get sidetracked, and to stay focused. The markets are volatile and you can't let market volatility and resulting mood swings get you off track. The way to do it is to set firm schedules and to stick to them as much as possible. Plus, raising capital *can't* be done on a drive-by basis. You must deliver value in every interaction to truly differentiate yourself. Just because you're ready to take the capital doesn't mean that your potential client is ready to make the allocation. You can't really control that. Make sure that you are delivering value, are seen as trustworthy, and that you have a definable, unique edge. When the client is ready, he or she will write the ticket.

Richard Wilson: Great advice there. I believe that what you just said there will be worth more than 10 times the cost of this book to anyone who is looking to raise more capital for their fund. Over 90 percent of the hedge funds I speak to are not in a life cycle or track record position to attract a third-party marketer, yet they would like to have an outside party complete their marketing for them. This is because they barely have time to do marketing and they are not marketers at heart. What happens is the portfolio manager or trader puts in three to five hours a week toward marketing and, like you said, this becomes a drive-by effort and not much capital is raised. I truly think that most hedge funds need to develop their own internal marketing resources, tools, processes, pipelines, and talent. That is how things finally get done in the majority of cases I have seen. Thanks for sharing that bit.

Do you have any other pieces of advice related to operational hedge fund best practices that you could share with other managers in the industry?

Pratik Sharma: This business is *all* about raising capital. That is not to say you can't get anywhere without performance, but what differentiates a hedge fund from a person trading in his gym shorts is the ability to raise capital. Invest your time and money accordingly.

HENDRIK KLEIN, CEO, DA VINCI INVEST LTD.

The final interview related to fund operations and institutionalization is with Hendrik Klein, CEO of Da Vinci Invest Ltd., a Zurich-based hedge fund professional whom I also interviewed for Chapter 2.

Richard Wilson: What have you learned that has enabled your firm to raise capital to this point where you are managing a healthy stable level of assets?

Hendrik Klein: It is challenging. Investors want liquidity, return, and no risk. Additionally, you should have a Goldman Sachs partner background with Harvard graduation.

Richard Wilson: I agree that pedigree is very important to investors regardless of their location. In the United States, and at least with my experience in working with UK-based groups, most institutional investors are demanding $80 million to $100 million or more in single strategies managed by fund managers. Is that what you have found as well?

Hendrik Klein: The fund volume should be above $50 million USD minimum, although $100 million USD would not hurt, and a three-year track record. The rest is a numbers game and the discipline to follow up on every lead in 24 hours.

Richard Wilson: How has your firm gotten past the "under $100 million, no institutional-quality operations" objection in the past? Gone to smaller investors who don't hold this objection? Met with investors face-to-face? Any lessons learned here?

Hendrik Klein: Cooperate with other asset managers, go to family offices, smaller funds of funds, and retail investors.

Richard Wilson: How long is your typical investor sales cycle? Eight months? Twelve months? Eighteen months?

Hendrik Klein: On average, our sales cycle for new investors is eight months.

Richard Wilson: What is the most valuable lesson you have learned while raising capital over the past few years?

Hendrik Klein: Follow up in 24 hours. Keep it simple.

Richard Wilson: What do you see as your main challenge in raising new capital for your hedge fund?

Hendrik Klein: Explaining our compelling strategy in a way so that investors feel comfortable to invest. Getting over the $50 million fund size with every fund that we offer.

Richard Wilson: What types of marketing materials do you use to market your fund to new potential investors? Anything really unique?

Hendrik Klein: Presentation, DDQ, fact sheet, references, press releases, articles in magazines.

Richard Wilson: Do you use a CRM system? How do you track important investor relationships or potential investor contact details?

Hendrik Klein: Yes, we use Salesforce, but we want to switch to Emnis in 2010.

 BONUS VIDEO MODULE

To watch a video on the components of a hedge fund marketing system, please type this URL into your Web browser: http://HedgeFundTraining.com/Marketing-System

---

CHAPTER SUMMARY

Tassini Capital Management was making several mistakes that emerging hedge funds often make. These mistakes included:

- Not strategically focusing on certain types of investors.
- Not developing a system to track investor pipeline development.
- Not developing or communicating an institutional-quality fund business while speaking with investor firms.

Discovering these flaws, thanks to their relationship with the third-party marketer, led to several changes. The most important of these included:

- Updating marketing materials.
- Obtaining investor databases.
- Focusing their investor prospects.
- Communicating a clear competitive advantage.
- Employing a multiple-modality marketing and sales approach.

This chapter covers many additional practical capital-raising best practices, unique positioning techniques being used by hedge funds today, and a hedge fund marketing case study. Here are some key lessons that can be taken from this chapter:

- Develop a list of 10 to 15 publications you wish your hedge fund would be featured in and approach them one by one.
- Write for audiences and speak at events full of prime prospects, not competitors.
- Despite the constant search, there is no person or resource that is a *real* shortcut to raising lots of capital for a hedge fund.
- To employ educational marketing, use folders, white papers, PowerPoint presentations, speaking, and writing, and focus on wealth management and financial planner markets.
- Use the "Four Why Tool" instead of constantly seeking new investors or larger investor databases.
- The difference between a $1 bill and $100 bill is the message on the paper. Don't underestimate the power of strong sales writing.
- Sales cycles for hedge fund investors may range from two to three months for high net worth investors to eight or more months for institutional investors.
- Webinars are a useful tool, and you *must* have a USP or you will be ignored.
- Use stories and personalized signatures and pictures in your marketing materials.
- At any one time, target 50 to 150 investor prospects per marketing and sales team member.

Free Resource: Learn more about hedge fund marketing at ThirdPartyMarketing.com.

REVIEW QUESTIONS

1. What percent of institutional investors will not invest unless they understand the investment being made?
   a. 55
   b. 44
   c. 78
   d. 88

2. While employing public relations tactics, target _____ publications in which you would aim to have your hedge fund or principal featured, and begin approaching them.
   a. 10 to 15
   b. 20 to 30
   c. 15 to 25
   d. 70 to 80
3. True or false: Somewhere around 50 percent of your competitors are probably ignoring copy writing best practices.
4. Hendrik Klein suggests that investors want liquidity, returns, and _____.
   a. Tax assistance.
   b. No risk.
   c. Advice.
5. True or false: Large service providers are always better as they provide more stable services and a more experienced team of professionals.
6. True or false: The "Four Why Tool" helps determine the real root cause of a problem so you can directly solve that instead of focusing on symptoms of a core issue your hedge fund is facing.
7. True or false: Multi-modality marketing material sets means having your marketing materials translated into at least two different languages each quarter.
8. The four main focuses of your PowerPoint presentation should be:
   a. Team pedigree, returns, transparency, and risk controls.
   b. Team pedigree, returns, financial controls, and risk controls.
   c. Team pedigree, experience, investment process, and risk controls.
9. Do not ever let your PowerPoint presentation reach more than _____ pages in length.
   a. 10
   b. 20
   c. 30
   d. 60
10. The most important part of your speeches, e-mails, or sales letter communications are the:
    a. Conclusions.
    b. Personalized style.
    c. Headlines and introductions.

Answers: To view the answers to these questions, please see http://HedgeFundTraining.com/Answers.

CHAPTER 4

The Shooting Star

The skills that get you out of Egypt are not the same skills that will bring you to the promised land.

—Joe Polish

This chapter focuses on managers of rapidly growing hedge funds, what they typically invest in, and what they do to keep the growth of their fund business moving forward. In this chapter, I touch on marketing tactics, reinvestment focus, and team building.

Why important: Fast-growing "shooting star" hedge funds have different needs, challenges, and opportunities than emerging hedge funds and giant $1 billion-plus hedge funds. The advice in this chapter is important because with consulting rates easily breaking $300/hour for this advice, most professionals do not freely give it away online or at many conferences or networking events.

18 LESSONS FROM SHOOTING STAR HEDGE FUNDS

Fast growing hedge funds are unlike most large and emerging hedge funds. These managers have figured something out and are positioned to grow, unlike more than 90 percent of the industry. Here are 18 lessons that can be taken away from some of the fast-growing hedge funds we have worked with:

1. They take transparency seriously and work to be proactively very transparent—more so than their competition. They take transparency into consideration from the investor's point of view.

2. They approach multiple investment channels but mostly ignore those completely out of their reach (for example, they ignore potential pension fund clients if they are running a $75 million fund).

3. They are always developing relationships and they have dedicated internal and some external professionals always selling on their behalf.

4. They not only seek pedigree on their team but they are always building that pedigree through additional research, hiring of expert staff, and through speaking and writing.

5. They document their operations and make decisions based on what is best long-term for the organization rather than what is cheaper to implement today. Like in any business, their ability to plan, strategize, and invest for the long-term forms a competitive edge for them in the industry.

6. They have risk management and trading plans which are closely followed. This helps them improve their actual trading results and provides confidence to investors since their historical trading actually matches up against the decision-making rules of their plans.

7. They know that "risk management," while sounding less sexy than "hedge funds," is the business they are in, and they invest in their own business accordingly.

8. They have documented, tested, and third-party-verified financial controls, compliance processes, and audits completed at least quarterly, and these reports are sent at least to board members if not also to investors.

9. They invest in and improve their infrastructure every year, even if the pay-off for doing so could be five to seven years away. Ironically, though, these are sometimes the investments that pay off the soonest because investors recognize the type of long-term investment being made.

10. They are experts at completing due diligence processes with institutional consultants, family offices, and other types of institutional investors. They have professionals who are trained for phone-based pitches and sales, and handoffs during these processes are seamless.

11. Their marketing materials are just as good as those of the $1 billion hedge funds because after investing $300,000 or more in infrastructure, talent, research, and risk management, it would be a waste not to spend $20,000 on presenting it in the right light in a professional manner.

12. They have seen the light that investing in the right areas does produce returns, so they reinvest their money even faster and often more efficiently than even small hedge funds on a tight budget.

13. They invest in training for their employees and board members with whom they grow longer-term relationships than many emerging hedge fund managers might.

14. They are not only aware of the competition but they are watching them—not in terms of what they are investing in so much as what risk management tools, software, trading tools, and USPs they are employing.

15. While hiring, they look for very specific skill sets and a minimum of seven years of experience in the industry, unless they have a policy of grooming from the ground up. Most fast-growing hedge funds I know, though, like to hire professionals who can hit the ground running and quickly integrate as part of the team. They actually have an HR department or at least one person who is head of talent development and HR-related activities, something almost all small hedge funds lack. When they are asked on the phone by institutional consultants if they plan on adding anyone to their team, they have a sophisticated, intelligent answer instead of the generic "We may add an analyst within the next three quarters."

16. They understand the "trust by verifying" mind-set of investors, and they make it easy to verify everything.

17. They conduct more due diligence on business partners, investors, and potential employees than some retail investors spend on investing in small emerging managed hedge funds.

18. They realize their success is never going to be built on one software program, capital-raising process, or investment trend, so they constantly are working to build their 1,000 blocks of competitive advantage and ability.

RICK NUMMI, PARTNER AND GENERAL COUNSEL, ACCOUNTING AND COMPLIANCE INTERNATIONAL (ACI)

This chapter's first interview is with Rick Nummi of ACI. Rick is a former senior attorney with the U.S. Securities and Exchange Commission (SEC) with expertise in enforcement and regulatory defense and compliance. He is a nationally recognized authority in securities law, regulation, and compliance, and is a featured speaker/educator at multiple industry (NRS, NSCP, NASD, SEC) trade conferences and presentations. Rick is also an experienced executive with a strong track record of helping registered representatives and broker-dealers succeed in a highly regulated industry.

Richard Wilson: Rick, first off, I know that hundreds of professionals pay to hear you speak at conferences, so I thank you for spending your time sharing some knowledge about what fast-growing hedge funds are doing here today with us.

Rick Nummi: My pleasure.

Richard Wilson: The focus of this chapter is a look into what fast-growing hedge fund managers who are growing assets quickly are doing. What do they invest in, what do they do differently? How are they growing their asset size even more? Do you have any unique insights that may not be mentioned anywhere else in this book related to these questions?

Rick Nummi: One of the things that we have seen is the utilization of the required annual review and the utilization of compliance reviews and sign-offs. Many times now we bind our annual review with our pedigree and background and provide it to their clients.

Richard Wilson: That is interesting; I have never heard of that happening before in the industry. How is this different from what your firm has experienced in the past while working with these same hedge fund clients?

Rick Nummi: Typically managers get these reports and sign-offs and hide them under their desk.

Richard Wilson: What has led to this drastic change?

Rick Nummi: Now some of these fast-growing managers are operating on the assumption that "nobody trusts anybody," and they take the perspective that while they simply do their internal review, they now need something more. Doing an internal review is somewhat like a BMW dealership salesman saying the car checks out and looks like it is ready to sell. These hedge fund managers would now like to show a signed-off document packet to potential investors.

Richard Wilson: Exactly what types of hedge funds are asking for this extra step—$1 billion-plus hedge funds? Hedge fund start-ups?

Rick Nummi: The primary differentiator here is that these are hedge fund managers who understand that you can be proactive with your operations and compliance and raise more capital by assuming that the general public and your investors do not trust anyone. The common thread that I find is that these fund managers are the ones who are raising the new capital. They are not all large or small, but they are effective at knowing what investors now really want from them.

Richard Wilson: Some fund managers I speak to shy away from institutionalization type discussions because they are already operating on a tight budget. Does this type of reporting include any extra costs?

Rick Nummi: No, there are no extra costs, really. It does not cost anything extra.

Richard Wilson: What happens if in your written report something is actually found? Then this transparent compliance strategy would backfire, wouldn't it?

Rick Nummi: Potentially, yes, but some of these clients request that problems are reported early so that they can be rectified before the report comes out. In this way, by the time the report becomes public, the issues have been addressed and handled.

Richard Wilson: This seems to be in line with the whole trend of institutionalizing your hedge fund regardless of how large it is. Do you see the institutionalization trend from your perspective?

Rick Nummi: Yes, very much so. The other twist is that the Investment Advisor Act itself requires self-compliance. The difference between non-successful clients and successful ones is that the fast-growing, shooting star funds take proactive steps to go past self-examination and take it to another level of sophistication and third-party verification.

Richard Wilson: Have you actually seen this help increase assets under management (AUM) for hedge fund managers?

Rick Nummi: Some funds that take these steps have done great during the recent economic and hedge fund downturn.

Richard Wilson: Do you have any other tips related to this proactive approach to becoming more transparent and then raising more capital because of it?

Rick Nummi: Yes. I often look at the track records and look at the hedge funds that are not growing and the ones that are really taking off in terms of assets, to see what makes one fund better than another fund. If you are asked for a risk management process, portfolio construction documentation, and sign-offs and you can't produce something in 24 hours, then it is obvious what type of fund or business you are running. Additionally, if you have completed all of the sign-offs and documentation yourself, that also shows evidence that you have not taken it seriously.

Richard Wilson: Great feedback.

Rick Nummi: What is most interesting about this is that many hedge fund managers will now eventually have to produce this report or sign-off on the fly. Investors may come in and say, "Before I invest, I want to see a document saying that this is taken care of and verified by a third party." This means that the cost of the proactive approach is almost exactly the same as the reactive one, except that there is no upside in being reactive. When you are reactive you look weak, and you don't stand out as being proactive to all of those other investors who do not explicitly ask for this level of documentation but who may still find comfort in it. It may be one of three things which really set your fund apart.

Traditionally, we have never had to place our pedigree right on our compliance reports. Lack of pedigree in the reports was an industry standard, but recently hedge fund managers have been asking me to put in my biography in the official report and review. Now, investors are judging the fund's pedigree directly and indirectly through their service providers.

BONUS VIDEO MODULE

To watch a video on the importance of pedigree and a strong team for hedge fund managers, please type this URL into your Web browser: http://HedgeFundTraining.com/Pedigree

Richard Wilson: I agree a hundred percent. I think the long-term difference that steps like this can make could make or break a business in this competitive industry.

Rick Nummi: We have many clients now come to us and say, "You worked for the SEC—what should we be taking seriously? What else could we be doing?"

Richard Wilson: Do you see any other trends in the actions of fast-growing or large hedge fund managers? These are often the most secretive.

Rick Nummi: We also do due diligence for two of the top five hedge funds in the United States. One of the interesting things that occurs when those funds identify an investment opportunity in another fund is that, absent a third-party review, those funds do not invest, ever. The institutional practices, justified or not, are being completed at all levels in all silos of the industry. The big institutional firms drive the marketplace, and they will take nothing at face value these days. They want everything complete and every detail checked at every single turn.

Richard Wilson: What else have you seen happening to fast-growing hedge funds lately in the industry?

Rick Nummi: The Madoff Effect. This is the client liquidating everything, taking all of their money out of the fund, and then immediately putting it back into the fund, just to see if they could do it.

Richard Wilson: That must be a relatively expensive experiment or risk management check.

Rick Nummi: They typically don't care if there are withdrawal penalties that add up to 5 to 10 percent of assets. They just want to know that it can be done. This is widespread with fast-growing small to medium-size hedge funds, and this is not slowing down; typically one or two investors per fund do this each year. When this is done they are really testing whether the fund can execute what it promises. What is interesting is that our firm and many firms like ours can validate this with an independent report for investors, but they don't want that—they want a real live check on the hedge fund manager.

These are smart people investing in hedge funds, and this circles back to our original point. The hedge fund managers who realize the public's mind-set are the ones who continue to grow at an astronomical rate. If you don't understand their gut feeling, you will not be successful. You could very well be the best stock reader on the planet, but if you don't understand the individual investor and what keeps them up at night you are sunk. Nobody is above scrutiny anymore. It doesn't matter how many assets under management you have, either.

Richard Wilson: That is interesting, because typically low AUM tends to be what holds small and emerging hedge fund managers back from becoming shooting star or giant hedge funds. While I know that demand and limitation have not been lifted, you wonder if this development will actually level the playing field, as some hedge funds do not have these proactive reports and checks in place and other small funds that have historically been ignored do. I think this may be an area of real opportunity for those funds looking to pass the $100 million or $250 million threshold and start working with more institutional firms.

Rick Nummi: I think you are correct in that assessment. In every challenge there is an opportunity.

Richard Wilson: That leads to a question that many hedge fund managers may be asking themselves when it comes to service provider partnerships. How do they know who they should hire in this space?

Rick Nummi: We have a tool on our web site which helps fund managers select compliance and regulation experts to work with. Here is an excerpt from this resource—16 questions that managers can use when they interview prospective service providers:

1. *Was your financial regulatory experience . . . in my type of firm?* Many compliance consultants attempt to dazzle you with their former regulatory titles. In many cases, their previous experience wasn't even in your type of firm, or even worse, they have no prior regulatory experience whatsoever. Make sure your prospective consultant has relevant experience in your type of firm.

2. *What level of financial regulator were you (examiner, branch chief, associate director, director)?* Just as in the first question, prior regulatory experience as an SEC investment adviser examiner does you no good if you are a broker-dealer. More importantly, experience as a former examiner doesn't give a big-picture view like more senior levels of regulatory management. Do not hire a firm without checking for the level of regulatory management expertise.

3. *How long ago were you a financial regulator?* Many consulting firms utilize long retired former regulators. The world has changed

considerably in the past year (just think of the changes over the past 5 to 10 years). Make sure your consultant has recent regulatory experience.

4. *When was the last conference you spoke at (that wasn't hosted by your firm)?* Many consultants tout their public speaking engagements as proof of competence. Make sure they let you know if the conference they spoke at was hosted by their own firm. Would you rather have an expert impartial consultant or someone trying to sell you a vacation?

5. *When did you get your law degree?* With the recent wave of regulatory changes, more and more consultants are unable to understand the legalese in which the new rules are written. If you hire a consultant, shouldn't he have the professional qualifications to explain the nuances of the law? Why wouldn't you want a consultant who is also a qualified lawyer and/or a certified public accountant (CPA)?

6. *How big was the firm where you were chief compliance officer (CCO)?* Again, many consulting firms have so-called experts who have never held senior positions at financial firms. Wouldn't it be nice to have someone who has walked in your shoes and understands your issues?

7. *What certifications do you hold as an auditor or examiner?* Your consulting firm should be required to have staff that is just as qualified as you are. Being an auditor or an examiner requires specialized training. Ask them what professional designations they hold that qualify them to do the work you require.

8. *How many active financial industry licenses does your staff hold?* Your consultant should have, at the very least, the same licenses you do. Ask them what they are and when they got them.

9. *How much finance or accounting experience do you have?* A consultant should be appropriately experienced in his/her field. Ask them how much experience they have, when, and who for. Hyperbole such as "120 years of experience" or "We have been around the longest" is meaningless if the company was bought or sold and/or key personnel have left. The better question is: "How much experience do *you* have?"

10. *What publications have quoted you on compliance topics?* Your consultant should be just as comfortable being quoted in the *Washington Post* or on CNBC as discussing the same issue with you. Most major media personnel understand the concept of credibility and why it is absolutely necessary before quoting someone. Ask your prospective consultant for their quotes. Most are justifiably proud of their appearances in the media. Conversely, if they have never been quoted, you may wonder why not.

11. *Do you write your own procedures manuals and, if so, why?* A consulting firm should be consulting, not creating products for sale. Your

firm is charged by law with crafting and editing procedures manuals. Every regulatory examiner can spot a canned boilerplate manual.

12. *How many fully qualified (in all areas: Investment Advisor, Broker-Dealer, hedge fund, banking) consultants do you have?* Many firms have consultants who are fully versed in only one area of the financial industry. Wouldn't you prefer a fully versed consultant, experienced and licensed across all relevant areas? Only through broad experience can a consultant assist you with fitting the disparate pieces together. Don't settle for less.

13. *At how many legal proceedings have you testified as an expert witness?* The legal system understands qualifications even better than you do. You must be certified as an expert in your field prior to the forum accepting your testimony. A good consultant will have testified (and been certified) many times. Ask them about the last time they testified.

14. *Precisely how many of each of these have you personally examined: Broker-Dealer, Investment Advisor, hedge fund, bank?* Make sure you get the consultant's scorecard. It is how consultants rate each other. It is also how you evaluate the depth of experience of your prospective consultant. An answer of 3-1-0-0 is not very comforting.

15. *How many existing (i.e., paid you in the past six months) clients do you have?* Many consulting firms advertise a large number of clients. However, just like in the financial services industry, things change. The more relevant question is "How many paid you last year?" You are required to carefully evaluate advertising. Choosing a consulting firm requires the same diligence to avoid exaggerated claims.

16. *Are you the consultant that will be assisting me?* Many firms will discuss all of the preceding questions generically—that is, "We have 99 lawyers, 4,000 clients, 55 CPAs," and so on. You want to know whether the 99 lawyers will all be assisting *you*. Actually, what you really want to know is, "What qualifications does *my* consultant have?" Also be wary of the bait and switch, or "We use a team approach," which translates to "We sold you X and we are giving you Y." The hiring of a consultant is an important decision. You should meet them, question them, and make sure the fit is good before agreeing to a long-term commitment.

Richard Wilson: Great questions to ask. Many of these questions could be rephrased to help fund managers hire other types of service providers and partners as well, so I will make sure and keep this in the main section of the book and not demote it to an appendix where it may be missed. Thank you for your time today, Rick.

Rick Nummi: Thank you for the opportunity, Richard.

THOMAS POWELL, CHIEF EXECUTIVE OFFICER, ELP CAPITAL

The next interview in this section on shooting star hedge funds is with Thomas Powell, chief executive officer of ELP Capital, a Nevada-based hedge fund. As chief strategist, Mr. Powell has combined his education and experience in commercial and retail banking, mortgage banking, real estate development, and corporate finance and governance to successfully lead the company through several periods of market growth and contraction. Mr. Powell also serves as the company's chief investment officer, helping to identify and structure investment vehicles creating solid investment options for ELP Capital Advisors' family of funds, institutional investors, and individual project investors.

Richard Wilson: What should very quickly growing hedge funds of $100 million invest their money in as they grow? What is most important?

Tom Powell: I believe there is nothing that dictates a company's success more than the quality of the individuals who make up its team. Investing in and attracting quality employees will continue to pay dividends throughout a company's life span.

Richard Wilson: I agree that pedigree and team are very important. In many capital market vehicles, whether it be private equity, hedge funds, venture capital, or angel investing, the team is the element that investors focus on most when deciding whether to get involved. Today's hedge fund industry has developed to the point where many managers can increase their team pedigree by hiring an outsourced CCO, building a strong board of advisers, or choosing authority service providers. There are many ways to grow a team.

Where do you see hedge funds slowing down their own growth due to lack of resources or skills? What mistakes do you see being made by very fast-growing $100 million-plus funds?

Tom Powell: Quality hedge funds are slowing down their growth in order to strengthen their systems and structures. Doing so enables successful funds to be highly efficient and helps them to prepare for the future. Putting priority on systems and structures can keep hedge funds operating consistently no matter how volatile market conditions may become.

Richard Wilson: What best practices do you see either shooting star hedge funds or giant $1 billion-plus hedge funds implementing that almost all small hedge funds ignore or discount?

Tom Powell: Big hedgers talk equally of both long- and short-term goals and strategies. Small funds are more centered around their short-term strategies and they communicate those targets. Such a short-term focus inevitably comes across in a fund's identity, and its managers lose focus on larger goals. The bigger funds, at least the successful ones, are able to think and act on a more global level.

Richard Wilson: This goes hand in hand with what we hear from Rick Nummi of ACI, that you have to speak with the same language and mindset as your investors. I believe that even if most institutional investors are sensitive to short-term volatility, they also have long-term investment horizons and global perspectives.

What insights do you have on the operational best practices or issues of these shooting star hedge funds like your own?

Tom Powell: Investors are now *demanding* that hedge fund firms be transparent. These difficult times have investors completing more prudent due diligence. In order to remain competitive in the marketplace, hedge fund managers have to be compliant and open with their processes. Transparency is by no means a new practice, but it has certainly gained importance in the minds of investors. Many hedge funds are employing name-brand, top-notch rating agencies to help highlight their dedication to being transparent.

Richard Wilson: I have heard from professionals of every type of hedge fund regarding the importance of transparency. This is obviously a hot button right now with investors. I want to acknowledge that while this advice is repeated in this text, I am not going to edit that out—I want to make sure its importance is not overlooked.

Everyone talks about the importance of institutional quality operations, but from your perspective, where should fast-growing hedge fund managers be reinvesting their money to improve their operations?

Thomas Powell: Without a doubt, hedge fund managers should be placing an emphasis on strengthening their systems and structures. This recession has badly shaken the investment world and now is the time to be building for (and adapting to) the future. Hedge fund managers must choose to either build the systems and structures internally or outsource the responsibility. Either way, they have to be operational and highly efficient. A fund can be producing phenomenal returns, and sales can be bringing in capital hand-over-fist, but without efficiency your customers will lose their trust and take their money elsewhere.

Richard Wilson: Great advice. Systems and structures of high-quality operations are as important to a fast-growing hedge fund as they are to any fast-growing business, yet small to medium-size hedge funds that I have spoken with rarely use flow charts, project managers, or hire operational consultants to streamline activities.

CHAPTER SUMMARY

Within this chapter on fast-growing hedge funds I interviewed experts who offer some advice, trends, and tips on what some of these fast-growing hedge funds are doing that may be different from both emerging hedge fund managers and giant $1 billion-plus hedge funds. Some key lessons from this chapter include the following:

- Some hedge funds are now asking for the pedigree of the service provider to be attached to every report, analysis, and sign-off, to assure investors that it is being completed by experts in the field.
- Rick Nummi suggests that the hedge funds he knows that are quickly gaining assets are those which realize that at some level "nobody trusts anybody." You must keep that in mind while making decisions on infrastructure, reporting, service provider selection, transparency, liquidity, and things like lock-up periods and gating clauses.
- Fast-growing hedge funds are prepared for and very responsive to investor demands for compliance or risk-reporting documentation.
- Talent is what one Nevada hedge fund CEO suggests as the most common element of a fast-growing hedge fund.

REVIEW QUESTIONS

1. Thomas Powell of ELP Capital believes that while returns and marketing are important, without _____ you will lose the trust of investors and fail as a business.
   a. A high pedigree team
   b. A web site
   c. Corporate quality real estate
   d. Operational efficiency
2. True or false: Recently transparency has become less important, because after Madoff most of the large frauds in the industry have been quickly uncovered.
3. One key difference between fast-growing and successful hedge funds and those that have not raised much capital is that the fast-growing hedge funds focus more on the _____ goals and less on the _____ goals.
   a. Long-term, short-term.
   b. Short-term, long-term.
   c. Capital-raising, operational.
   d. Capital-raising, compliance.

4. Investors reward those hedge funds with proactively _____ with respect to capital allocations.
   a. Aggressive capital-raising strategies.
   b. Fast-growing teams.
   c. Transparent operations.

5. Rick Nummi suggests that those hedge fund managers who understand _____ will grow at an astronomical rate compared to others with similar opportunities.
   a. The political nature of investments.
   b. The mind-sets of investors.
   c. The laws preventing certain types of investments.
   d. The taxes that affect hedge fund investments.

6. What is referred to as the Madoff Effect within this chapter is the practice of investors:
   a. Demanding quarterly fraud checks.
   b. Completely liquidating their assets within the fund.
   c. Asking for hedge funds to start using independent administration firms.
   d. Requiring most hedge funds to have an in-house chief compliance officer.

7. Many hedge funds try to be too _____ to investor demands when really they could have an edge and improve their whole business by being more _____.
   a. Large to meet, small business-like.
   b. Reactive, aggressive.
   c. Reactive, proactive.
   d. Aggressive in raising capital and working, patient.

Answers: To view the answers to these questions, please see http://HedgeFundTraining.com/Answers.

CHAPTER 5

Hedge Fund Start-Up Guru

I hated every minute of training, but I said, "Don't quit. Suffer now and live the rest of your life as a champion."

—Muhammad Ali

Thousands of hedge funds are started each year, but not all survive. Many start-ups are stopped in their tracks before they ever begin trading the portfolio. This chapter provides some hedge fund start-up-related tips as well as interviews with hedge fund start-ups that have survived and succeeded in hiring, raising capital, and operating for several years. In this chapter managers share lessons they have learned, what they wish others had told them before launching, and their top tips for emerging hedge fund managers.

Why important: Over 1,000 hedge funds are launched each year. Despite this high level of competition, most hedge funds repeat the same mistakes as they launch their businesses. This is not necessarily the fault of the hedge fund manager, because information on starting a fund is sparse and often only provided by firms with a strong vested interest in directing your hard-earned dollars toward their bank accounts. Through this chapter you will be able to quickly pick up valuable lessons from those who have started and grown their hedge funds, and worked with thousands of fund manager start-ups.

 BONUS VIDEO MODULE

To watch a video on wow to start a hedge fund, please type this URL into your Web browser: http://HedgeFundTraining.com/Start-A-Hedge-Fund

TOP FIVE TIPS FOR STARTING A HEDGE FUND

I recently completed a consulting engagement with a group of professionals who wanted my most concise tips on how they should launch and start their hedge fund, what they should focus on, and what expectations they should have. Here are some of my pieces of advice to them.

1. Starting a hedge fund is not a get-rich-quick scheme. In 90 percent of the cases our firm has witnessed, it takes at least three to five years before the hedge fund becomes profitable and stable as a business. I've worked with a client in the past who had been running a fund for seven years and still had not raised enough capital to be self-sustaining.

2. Always complete due diligence on your service providers. I know of a hedge fund manager who, in 2009, was given a quote of more than $80,000 for some very simple legal formation costs, which is at least $35,000 above what most other firms charge for this same service. If new hedge funds do not shop around, they could end up paying twice as much to service providers as they need to. No, hedge fund start-ups should not select service providers based on price—but they should always sit down or have conference calls with at least three prime brokerage firms, three auditors, and three administration firms before deciding who to work with.

3. Always be growing relationships. This is not the same as "always be selling." Selling can be spotted from five suits away at a networking event, and felt in how someone asks what company you work for and what your role is there. It is always best to take the high road, the long-term approach, yet always be looking for those individuals whom you should invest a significant portion of your time getting to know. The benefits of doing so could be valuable advice, leads, or an allocation. If you are always looking too closely, then no professionals along the way will want to give you feedback on your marketing materials or suggest an alternative path to raising assets.

4. Focus on risk management and the investment process more than on high performance returns. Yes, investors want to see strong returns, but a top-five sign of a green hedge fund manager is someone who constantly pushes his extremely high returns found in back-testing or his first four months of operating. Doing so ruins your chance of serious consideration as it gives off the impression that your fund will reach for those returns at any cost or risk. Speaking about returns too much detracts from confidence in your fund's investment process and risk management controls.

5. Invest in yourself. Choose high-quality service providers. Build a team. Break down your investment process into concrete steps, and spend

50 hours creating a solid PowerPoint presentation/pitch book for your fund. Don't show it to a single investor until you have completed five drafts of it. Too many times I see hedge fund managers looking to raise capital who have not yet taken the time to organize their own thoughts, plans, or marketing materials. If your hedge fund is not worth your own investment of time, why should anyone else invest their time and possibly capital into it? Investors look for signs of a manager having skin in the game in multiple ways.

Most hedge fund start-ups I speak with want referrals to respected service providers or advice on attracting seed capital. Almost none have a business plan for their hedge fund and only a few have PowerPoint presentations explaining their investment strategy. If you are a fund manager in this position, that doesn't mean you have done anything wrong, but you may consider writing both a hedge fund business plan and a comprehensive 15- to 25-page PowerPoint presentation now to make it easier to work with service providers, third-party marketers, institutional consultants, and potential investors.

Your hedge fund business plan should include information about the following:

- *Management.* What team members are required to run the fund effectively? What is the chain of command? How are decisions made? What happens if two or three professionals disappear tomorrow? Who would take over responsibilities and what would happen to your investors' funds? The importance of a well-constructed and well-managed team cannot be overstated.
- *Investment process and risk management.* Managing risk is what running a hedge fund is all about. Meet with your prime brokerage firm's risk advisory division, speak with your traders and portfolio managers, and network with other managers to pick up some best practices in this space. At the end of the day, your risk management approach, investment process, and team must be molded into one cohesive group all pointed in the right direction. There is no magic bullet to raising assets or gaining seed capital, but getting this combination right is the most important thing you can focus on.
- *Service providers.* Who are you going to use as your prime brokerage firm, fund administrator, auditor, or third-party marketer? How will this evolve as your fund passes the $100 million and $300 million marks? Will you use multi–prime brokerage services? Capital introduction teams? Multiple third-party marketers? Your choice of firms in this space can affect the levels of assets you manage, the quality of advice you receive, and the reputation of your firm as a whole. My

advice would be to meet and interview at least three service providers of each type in person or over several phone calls, and go with one that is well experienced yet not so large that your sub–$1 billion account is an annoyance to them.

■ *Infrastructure and technology.* Meet with other local hedge fund managers, your trader, your prime brokerage firm, and other service providers to nail down exactly what you will need in terms of reporting, processing, and functioning not only as a hedge fund but as a small business. When you start a hedge fund you become an entrepreneur, and you have to face all of the challenges that accompany that distinction in addition to those challenges found in managing your portfolio. Many funds underestimate the costs of some of the technology needed to operate as they grow beyond the simple $1 to $5 million fund operations.

■ *Marketing.* Nothing is traded or managed until the dollars come in. Anyone who joins your firm or board will want to know how you plan to grow your business. What channels of investors will you approach—institutional investors including funds of hedge funds, consultants, large family offices, pension funds or smaller family offices, wealth management firms, high net worth (HNW) individuals, and accredited investor clubs? Here is a hint: In our asset-raising experience, the latter should be 80 percent of your focus if you are managing less than $100 million. What resources do you or should you have in place to meet these goals? Third-party marketers? Databases of investors? An in-house marketing specialist? How much does this cost and when should these resources be put in place?

HEDGE FUND PITCH BOOK CREATION

Following is a list of tips for professionals looking to create a pitch book for their hedge fund. My advice to both $90 million and $1 million hedge funds is that you can never start this process too early. It is an iterative and constantly evolving project which will never be complete. Here are the top 10 tips for creating hedge fund marketing materials.

1. Think long-term. Invest in creating a robust, institutional-quality pitch book the first time around, and complete five drafts of it internally before showing it to a single investor.
2. Emphasize the strengths of your team, investment process, and risk management controls and how they all interact inside the operations of your hedge fund.

3. Make your competitive advantage clear and do not rely on canned phrases such as "positive returns in bull or bear markets." Anyone who reviews hedge fund materials for a living will see these by the hour. Your advantage must be unique.

4. Stress the importance and individual functions of the team, their experiences, and their pedigree. This should be the foundation upon which everything else is built.

5. Do not send any pitch book or marketing material out before speaking with a qualified compliance or legal counsel on the team.

6. Create a one-page marketing sheet, a PowerPoint presentation of 13 to 20 or more slides, and a one-page newsletter which would be released monthly providing your view of the markets in your niche area of expertise.

7. Work with high-caliber service providers so that you don't draw extra skepticism as a relatively new fund, which may already be receiving extra scrutiny by potential investors and advisers.

8. Use your whole team, your prime brokerage business partners, and other service providers to improve your marketing materials. Professionals who work in prime brokerage or administration see many types of marketing materials and can help provide valuable feedback at no additional cost to your fund.

9. Do not create a PowerPoint presentation that is longer than 30 slides. There are some institutional money managers who run three similar funds and will sometimes cover each of these in a single presentation, but this is the exception. Ninety-five percent of the people to whom you will send the PowerPoint presentation will not read more than 15 pages of the material unless you are walking them through it over the phone or in person.

10. Purchase the rights to graphics; choose a unique, simple, professional layout for the presentation; and use the newest software diagramming tools to create an institutional-quality presentation. Coming into a meeting with a Word document or 25 pages of bullet points is not very effective. It is hard enough to catch investors' attention and bring them to the table to discuss your fund. You don't want to lose them due to the aesthetics of your PowerPoint.

SYED ALI, CEO, SATURN PARTNERS, LLC

For this chapter I interviewed Syed Ali, CEO of Saturn Partners, LLC. I have had a relationship with Syed for close to two years, first starting as a consultant to help his company update their marketing materials and most recently by joining their advisory board as a business development adviser. I sat down with Syed to have him share his story of how he started his hedge fund.

Richard Wilson: I speak with lots of professionals who want to start one but they are not sure if they have the "right" background. How exactly did you get to start your own hedge fund?

Syed Ali: I found a passion in trading when I saw an ad in a commodities magazine. I initially started trading in silver futures and lost the entire $10,000 I had saved diligently. At that time I was in part-time management at UPS and would make my trades on a phone while I was supervising my crew, and at that time there were no cell phones. Shortly thereafter my manager wanted me to get into full-time management, but a requirement then was that everyone had to drive a delivery package car for a period of time. So I saved up $75,000 over time and was trading silver, orange juice, sugar, and the grains. It was a good thing I was single at that time. The only way I could trade back then was using all the pay phones on my delivery route. Looking back, it certainly was amazing I delivered all the packages in a timely manner. I went through more hardships and lost all the money.

Richard Wilson: That must have been a humbling experience.

Syed Ali: This was a very humbling experience but I still had a passion for trading. I then met a person named Don M., and that was a turning point in my life. Since he had the financial means, he suggested that I trade for him. I traded stocks and it took a few more years to develop our methodology. This man is one of the most patient and honorable people I have ever known. We decided to start a hedge fund so we could reap some of the rewards for all the work that was put into our system.

Richard Wilson: So when did you actually launch your hedge fund?

Syed Ali: We started trading operations in November 2006 as a long/short equity fund. Leading up to this we hired a law firm to do our private placement memorandum (PPM), and then we had to get an accountant and shortly thereafter an auditor. We did this as we went along, hoping to avoid any land mines. Since we had a positive year in 2006 and 2007, we thought that it would be a little easier raising funds, but that was not the case. I made contact with the person at my brokerage firm at the end of 2007 to see if he could be of assistance in raising funds, but he did not have a decent platform. In June 2008, through the help of our auditor, we switched brokerage firms since they had a good platform in raising my assets under management (AUM).

Although 2008 was a tough year for us and many others, we had a gain for the year. I was relieved because I don't think I slept from September

2008 to December 2008, and that had to be the toughest period I had encountered. With all the turmoil in the markets, it looked very grim for our fund in raising AUM, since redemptions were the only game in town. I was hoping that things would change toward the latter part of 2009. Let me say this, that along the way there were many people who helped us, and that is an essential ingredient to survivability.

Richard Wilson: So what have you learned the hard way by launching your own hedge fund that you wish someone had told you before you started your hedge fund business? What lessons could you share with others now starting hedge funds?

Syed Ali: Since I do not live in a large city, it was tough to get certain questions answered in relation to launching a hedge fund since there were many local professionals who had no idea what a hedge fund was about. Actually our first accountant had to educate himself on hedge fund accounting. I wished I was connected to a network of informed individuals who could have walked me through the process. I wished that someone had informed me that it was going to be a tough road and that just having good returns was not the only factor in raising funds. Completing the Certified Hedge Fund Professional (CHP) Designation Program by the Hedge Fund Group helped; the articles, required readings, and video content give valuable information for those starting funds. The CHP helps with credibility, foundational industry knowledge, and the ability to speak the industry language.

 BONUS VIDEO MODULE

To watch a video on the importance of hedge fund training, please type this URL into your Web browser: http://HedgeFundTraining.com/Online

---

Richard Wilson: While I know that some cities such as New York, London, and Geneva are famous for housing thousands of hedge funds, I have spoken with hundreds of funds in Alaska, Egypt, Sydney, Moscow, and São Paulo in similar situations as you were. I think that identifying proper advisers and consultants along the way is critical to keep you on a straight path; sometimes the wrong service providers can cost you years of time and possibly even the viability of your business. Do you have any other advice related to service providers that you learned along the way?

Syed Ali: Yes, we also learned that it was important to have a knowledgeable law firm that not only can help with a PPM but could guide one through the many pitfalls of what can or cannot be disclosed or said. Also, having a multipartner accounting firm as a hedge fund administrator to put investors at ease and possibly guide you to grow organically.

Richard Wilson: What if you had just one piece of advice you wanted a hedge fund manager to take away from this interview? What should they keep in mind and remember each day while running their business?

Syed Ali: Continue to post returns with minimum drawdowns. This is probably the most important advice I can give anyone. Be patient. Do not risk too much on one company or event. Anticipate and do not react. If you are unsure, get out. Make sure you find an established hedge fund administration firm and law firm that have a good platform for them to help you grow out your infrastructure. The hardest thing I learned was to control drawdowns. This is a must in the first three years, which are the most critical.

Richard Wilson: That is great advice. I actually hear a mirror of that advice from investors often. Most investors have little patience for volatile returns. Wealth management and family office investors especially have a hard time explaining to their end HNW or ultra high net worth (UHNW) investors why their portfolio might fluctuate, and this can lead to redemptions. I think your advice here is in line with my experience that the stability of solid performance is one of the top three things investors look for. How long did it take you to launch your hedge fund?

 BONUS VIDEO MODULE

To watch a video called "What Is a Family Office?" please type this URL into your Web browser: http://HedgeFundTraining.com/Family-Office

---

Syed Ali: It took us six months to launch our fund from start to finish. We formed our fund around an LLC and the total cost of doing so was $25,000.

Richard Wilson: I think that is important to share. I often see two extremes in the industry. Either hedge funds pay $80,000 to $120,00 or more for more simple types of fund formation services when they could get the same services for $30,000 to $60,000 from another experienced firm, or managers see this cost as unneeded and they try to find someone to form their fund for $2,000 or less. Most of the hedge fund experts and consultants I work with agree on $15,000 to $60,000 being what most hedge funds need to spend to retain quality legal advisory services while forming their funds. The more complicated the structure, the more expensive this part of the start-up process tends to be. What was the most difficult part of this formation process for you?

Syed Ali: The most difficult part for me was understanding all of the documents to the hedge fund, such as the PPM, and being knowledgeable enough to speak with investors and discuss the different sections of the documents.

Richard Wilson: What do you see as the main challenge of running a hedge fund today?

Syed Ali: The main challenge I see is reestablishing trust and being as transparent as possible, in light of market conditions and fraud. I also feel that it's very challenging to get to the next step from being a one-man or one-woman shop into broadening out the infrastructure into a real business.

Richard Wilson: I agree. I believe that having the right pedigree on your team, an audited track record by a well-known firm, an independent board, and great service providers can help investors hedge against this fraud risk to some degree. These are moving from the nice-to-have box to the must-have box quickly. What do you believe is helping you raise assets right now?

Syed Ali: I feel that being in as many databases online as possible, developing great marketing materials, and using the type of capital-raising articles and advice you provide with an in-house team is what is needed to grow an emerging hedge fund.

Richard Wilson: What types of marketing materials do you currently use?

Syed Ali: We have a one-page marketing PDF that summarizes our strategy and performance. We then also have a detailed 26-page PowerPoint presentation which covers our team, investment principles, investment process, risk management processes, performance, terms, and service providers. We have poured a lot of time into this one document and it is the key tool we use to market our fund to new investors.

Richard Wilson: Thank you for your time and sharing what you have learned while growing your hedge fund. I'm sure this will be helpful to many others who hope to follow this same path at some point.

Syed Ali: Thank you.

NAKUL NAYYAR, QUANTITATIVE
TRADING/SUPPORT, QUAD CAPITAL

My next interview was completed with Nakul Nayyar, an expert in trading who works for a U.S.-based hedge fund manager; he was also interviewed in Chapter 2.

Richard Wilson: What would you say are the top four most common or dangerous trading-related mistakes of hedge fund start-ups or emerging hedge fund managers?

1. I think all parties are aware on a certain level that the immediate results are of vital psychological importance. Though the fund may have been marketed for longer-term performance, investors are watching your first performance reports with a lot of interest. Although it's next to impossible to time your returns, it is important that managers stay focused and disciplined on risk management and specifically on avoiding drawdowns early on. The excitement and pleasure of performing well early on can create overconfidence, overselling, and overhype, which could work adversely. Conversely, poor performance can lead to undisciplined or revenge trading, which obviously can have negative consequences. Practical advice is to play small, put some green on the screen, and most importantly to get the investors comfortable with you as a manager and your trading style.

2. Don't be afraid to start small. One doesn't need to start a fund with $100 million, the best accounting and auditing, and spacious offices. Look seriously at a managed-account structure to start. These offer low start-up costs, transparency, and reporting through the broker. Don't put the cart in front of the horse; your absolute main goal at start-up is to deliver the performance that was marketed. Once track record and performance are established, the capital will come. If your strategy involves illiquid or hard-to-value (read: non-exchange-traded) assets, then consider the private equity route as opposed to a hedge fund.

3. Proprietary trading and hedge fund trading are different animals. At the risk of making generalizations, it has been my experience that prop traders usually emphasize absolute return giving a certain amount of risk. Hedge fund traders, by contrast, emphasize risk-adjusted performance, primarily because most investors do as well. Additionally, prop traders are allowed large latitudes in terms of strategy, whereas a hedge fund trader may be constrained to a specific approach of asset class.

These are extremely important distinctions and should not be taken lightly.

4. Failing to differentiate your fund in a mountain of other similar funds is another big mistake. You have highlighted this a few times at Hedge-FundBlogger.com and through your Hedge Fund Group. Networking and contacts are usually the best methods to attract capital in early stage start-ups. However, if a fund is forced to utilize more traditional challenges, then remember to account for the other 100 or more firms that also boast an impressive track record, low risk, diversification, and so on, that you outline in your marketing approach. The topic of differentiation should be of primary focus in the funds marketing plan.

Richard Wilson: I agree. Paying close attention to drawdowns and positions that are bleeding is something I hear traders refer to often. I think that watching your month-to-month performance is more important any other metric or time frame, really. Even seven-year track records get broken down to the month-to-month level of scrutiny and curiosity.

Can you suggest four best practices or valuable trading lessons learned through all of your experience? These lessons could be related to working on a trading team, using the right trading tools, developing your own system, cutting losses, and so on.

Nakul Nayyar: Sure, here are my top four best practices or best pieces of trading-related advice that I can provide:

1. Risk management is everything. There are a thousand and one reasons to enter a trade, but once the money is on the table, none of those reasons matter. This was an important lesson in my evolution as a trader. Unfortunately, the preponderance of books, articles, blogs, and pseudo mentors usually focus primarily on your entry criteria. It's sexy and it sells; risk management is not. If you read interviews of great traders and investors, you will hear everyone talk about risk and not some fancy entry rules. Warren Buffett: "Rule number 1: Never lose money. Rule number 2: Never forget rule number 1." George Soros: "My approach works not by making valid predictions but by allowing me to correct false ones." Bruce Kovner: "In real estate, it's location, location, location. In money management, it's risk management, risk management, risk management." Get the point?

2. Understand behavioral finance and especially biases about money. Although understanding some of the biases involved in a trading decision will not guarantee you will avoid these pitfalls, being cognizant that they exist is the best hedge available. Even quantitative traders can benefit greatly from understanding behavioral finance. One such benefit

is idea generation, as investor psychology can create inefficiencies. Another benefit is to help traders understand their own inherent biases in system testing such as excessive curve fitting, constant interference with executions, fiddling with or changing parameters, or marrying a strategy. Quant trading eliminates one set of biases for a complete set of new ones.

3. Try to maintain a trading log as detailed as possible, especially when starting a new strategy. If at all possible, paper-trade for a while. This log will be very important once you start comparing real-time statistics to historical or back-tested results. Additionally, a trading log will force you to look closely at individual trades. When trading a strategy, it is important to understand how and why your edge exists and to learn from experience when it works and when it doesn't.

4. To quantitative traders, fit the security to the model, not the model to the security. You will be glad you did. In other words, if you are researching mean-reversion trading, look at securities with a mean-reversion tendency. Similarly with trend following: QCOM will behave very differently from BIDU. This should free up some time to work on your portfolio allocation, which is far more important anyway.

Richard Wilson: What types of risk management tools have you found most effective while trading?

Nakul Nayyar: I would name three tools as most effective in risk management:

1. Options are securities designed for risk management. The interesting thing about options is the ability to design a risk-to-reward criterion before the trade is made. I have met many traders who utilize options as a leverage tool and not as risk management. Though it is one of the uses, I believe that notion is misplaced.

2. A complete trading plan with levels of entry, exits, contingencies, and so on, is an effective risk management tool that many either get complacent or too lazy to follow through on. When something is in writing it is much more difficult to rationalize away our initial ideas on the trade.

3. Having someone else, a competent risk manager perhaps or co-worker, review and monitor positions can be highly beneficial. We are constantly fighting our biases in this game and a fresh pair of eyes and opinions can allow the trader to reanalyze the situation. Oftentimes a trader will go for a walk, step away from it for a while, which allows them to regain perspective.

Richard Wilson: How do you see hedge fund trading and the industry changing over the next few years? Do you see the use of models and black box trading fading away or remaining strong in certain parts of the industry? Or maybe the industry is trading in more international markets than ever before? What trends are you seeing from your perspective?

Nakul Nayyar: I can name three basic trends:

1. In the quantitative trading space, I see a commoditization of the ultra-high-frequency space. It has been termed an "arms" race and, as such, that space will soon be dominated by the largest, most capitalized players. For example, at one point, triangular arbitrage was a strategy that once was lucrative but now is no longer a viable strategy for a majority of market players. It is obviously still being done, but participants will be forced to move further out of the risk curve and place more focus on forecasting over arbitrage.
2. There is also a very clear bifurcation in the hedge fund space based on liquidity of the strategy. Hedge funds will focus more on exchange-traded and liquid products, and those strategies that trade in illiquid or hard-to-value assets will likely choose a private equity formation.
3. Obviously there is more emphasis on transparency and investors' access to their capital, so operational requirements will become a vital part of a hedge fund business. Many hedge funds, especially start-ups, will look for more turnkey approaches or, more appropriately, a managed account structure.

CHAPTER SUMMARY

This chapter contains a great deal of advice, stories, and tips on how to both start a hedge fund and grow an emerging hedge fund. If you are looking to someday start a hedge fund, or are in charge of marketing an emerging hedge fund manager, this chapter may have been the most valuable one for you within this book. Some of the key lessons included in this chapter:

- Most hedge funds need at least three to five years to raise enough capital to create a sustainable business.
- Complete thorough due diligence on your service providers; have at least a short two- to three-page request for proposal (RFP) for them to complete while you are deciding who to work with going forward.
- Invest in yourself, your processes, infrastructure, service providers, hedge fund training, and relationships. Others prefer to invest with you or after you, not before you have built a strong business system.

- While creating your pitch book think long-term, stress your unique selling proposition (USP), use service providers and compliance advisers to improve the presentation, stress your team, and use a graphic designer or sales copy writer if you don't have those skills in-house.
- Syed Ali offers advice for emerging hedge fund managers: Watch draw-downs, don't overcorrect, and be very patient while building your track record.
- Nakul Nayyar recommends that emerging hedge fund managers should be unafraid to start small, have systematic risk management in place, create a complete trading plan, always maintain a trading log, and understand behavioral finance.

Free Resource: Learn more about hedge fund start-ups at HedgeFund StartupGuru.com.

REVIEW QUESTIONS

1. True or false: Nakul Nayyar suggests that you create a detailed trading plan so that you can take more aggressive positions within the portfolio and have those moves documented on paper within the firm.
2. True or false: Having someone else review your trades, look at your risk levels, and analyze your positions can be beneficial. This can bring new perspective to everything that is going on within the portfolio.
3. Above everything else, _____ is most important, even more important than _____ for trades.
    a. Risk management, entry points.
    b. Entry points, risk management.
    c. Trading logs being updated, risk management.
    d. Trading logs being updated, trading plans.
4. Within this chapter it is suggested that _____ should be the focus above all else while marketing a fund.
    a. Transparency.
    b. Operations.
    c. Differentiation.
    d. Outsourcing.
5. True or false: One difference between prop traders and hedge fund managers is that prop traders are allowed large latitudes in terms of strategy, whereas a hedge fund trader may be constrained to a specific approach of asset class.

6. True or false: Syed Ali believes that putting your fund into as many hedge fund research databases as possible is a bad idea and can hurt the brand of your hedge fund for two main reasons.
7. The two main challenges that Syed Ali and many emerging hedge fund managers face is moving up the learning curve on all of the legal and industry terms in the industry. The other main challenge is moving from a _____ to a _____ .
   a. Small start-up hedge fund, fund of hedge fund business.
   b. Small start-up hedge fund, $10 billion-plus fund within two years.
   c. Small start-up hedge fund, service provider to other hedge funds.
   d. Small start-up hedge fund, more established hedge fund business with proper infrastructure in place.
8. Which of the following is *not* suggested as a way to both address fraud risk and lower investor fears of this type of risk:
   a. Create an independent board of advisers.
   b. Employ trusted service providers and business providers.
   c. Ensure you employ a high-pedigree, experienced team.
   d. Have respected office space in either New York City or London.
9. True or false: Within this chapter we suggest to forget building relationships until you have a solid track record, team, and a great infrastructure in place—otherwise you will end up wasting your time and resources.
10. It is recommended that you do not show an investor your marketing documents or information on your fund until it has been reviewed at least __ times by your team of service providers.
    a. 3
    b. 5
    c. 10
    d. 15

Answers: To view the answers to these questions, please see http://HedgeFundTraining.com/Answers.

CHAPTER 6

Dedicated to Due Diligence

It is the studying that you do after your school days that really counts. Otherwise, you know only that which everyone else knows.

—Henry Doherty

*(**T**his chapter was written by Gregory Schink, a wealth management professional who helped lead the efforts to create the CHP Designation Level 2 Program on due diligence.)*

From the late 1990s through the third quarter of 2007, investors felt an overwhelming confidence in the validity of the investments they were selecting, and more especially the managers who ran them. Bernard L. Madoff Investment Securities had been brought up to the SEC for possible violations since as early as 1999. The SEC was alerted to possible fraud concerning Sir Allen Stanford as early as 2002. The credit crunch of 2007 was what finally brought these frauds to light.

The possibility of fraud going undetected on such a massive scale has caused a revolution in how in-depth due diligence will go when investigating a hedge fund and its manager(s) for potential investors. The days of run-and-gun investing when investors were chasing the highest returns possible (think Long Term Capital Management) are gone. Hedge funds must be crystal clear on their backgrounds, the processes they use, and the style they intend to implement. This is helping bring hedge funds more into the mainstream and change the public's opinion of how secretive they have appeared in the past, as well as making quality due diligence a must for high net worth (HNW) investors looking to invest in the hedge fund arena.

Why important: Due to recent scandals, media attention, fraud, and insider trading cases, due diligence is one of the most important topics in the industry. This is because due diligence is the forum through which fund managers may communicate their transparency, proactive institutional-quality operations, and robust investment process. It is also important because it is the method through which accredited and institutional investors attempt to avoid funds that may be more likely to be involved in scandals, fraud, blowups, or insider trading cases. If you are not aware of best practices and trends in the due diligence space, you may miss opportunities to manage risk or obtain additional capital.

In this chapter, the interviews Gregory completed with two prominent experts in the due diligence arena and Richard Wilson consisted of a series of questions to gain a further understanding of their experience in the due diligence field. The questions include personal background questions such as what is the preferred background for someone who wishes to start a profession in the due diligence arena concerning hedge funds; and what's the best advice you can give to someone starting out in due diligence. We also examine some due diligence best practice tips that each interviewee has, such as some telltale signs of a shady manager/fund, and what resources a hedge fund manager should have in place in order to efficiently move through a due diligence questionnaire (DDQ) process more efficiently.

Through each interview, we present three different backgrounds, opinions, and approaches to successful due diligence. Each individual has his own method of performing successful due diligence, but there are underlying similarities that are consistent across the due diligence domain that must be highlighted.

SCOTT FREUND, PRESIDENT, GCC FAMILY WEALTH MANAGEMENT

For this chapter's first interview, I spoke with Scott Freund, president of GCC Family Wealth Management. Scott graduated with a bachelor of science degree in mechanical engineering from Virginia Tech in 1991. Scott's investment background began with a boutique investment bank in Bethesda, Maryland, in 1994, and then in 1996 he moved to the private client group at Wheat First Butcher Singer (now Wachovia Securities). In 1999, Scott became a senior consultant with the Investment Consulting Services Group of Morgan Stanley. He was one of the first advisers at Morgan Stanley to earn the Certified Investment Management Analyst (CIMA) designation, and was also a Rule 144 specialist.

Scott joined the Private Bank at Bank of America in 2003 as a senior vice president and private client adviser, dealing not only with individuals and families, but with family offices as well. Working with the gatekeepers of these family offices served as a stepping-stone for the foundation, in July

2005 in Bethesda, Maryland, of Family Office Research, a multifamily office founded to provide objective advice as well as a higher level of customization and customer service for high net worth clients.

GCC Family Wealth Management was formed as a result of a merger with Family Office Research. It is a multifamily office designed to manage the complex wealth of a limited number of high net worth individuals, families, and foundations. GCC Family Wealth Management is a collaboration of expertise from different wealth management disciplines, including investment management, private banking, estate planning, insurance advisory, and risk management.

Scott Freund's recommendation for someone pursuing a job in the due diligence field is to gain knowledge in the legal, accounting, or investment arenas. He believes that good due diligence requires a very thorough individual who takes nothing at face value, and he implements the "don't trust and definitely verify" philosophy into his practice. He also thinks that due diligence is better performed by a fiduciary adviser as opposed to an adviser who works on a commission basis.

On average, Scott spends three to six months on a due diligence report for a single fund. It's mandatory to have background checks done on all principals involved in the fund during this stage. Some telltale signs that something may be amiss are if a manager is too quick to close or if he says they "need the money right away." On the flip side, trustworthy managers are always willing to let you speak with their auditors, attorneys, and shareholders and will encourage you to do so. Scott believes in the importance of checking on the status of the board of directors of each fund. This includes getting the telephone numbers of each member and verifying that each one of them is still associated, is proud to continue that association, and whether they are getting compensated in any way for being on the board of directors for the said fund.

One of the best standard due diligence questionnaires (DDQs) available comes from the Investment Management Consultants Association (IMCA). Scott believes that if fund managers would provide a DDQ (see Appendix B) and background checks to the due diligence team, it would streamline the entire process; they're going to find out, regardless.

BRIAN REICH, PRESIDENT AND FOUNDER, ATRATO ADVISORS LLC

For our second interview with a due diligence expert, I spoke with Brian Reich, president and founder of Atrato Advisors LLC. Brian holds a bachelor of science degree from Cornell University (1996) and a master's degree in business administration (2001) from the Stern School of Business at New York University. Prior to business school, Brian worked as a strategy consultant focused on the health care sector. He began his investment career at Salomon Smith Barney in the Derivatives Capital Markets Group. He then served as a senior research analyst and Investment Committee member at Richcourt Fund Advisors, the fund-of-funds business previously owned by the Citco Group.

Later, Brian was named the director and global head of hedge fund research for Deutsche Bank's private wealth management division. At Deutsche Bank, Brian oversaw the construction, development, and manager selection for the bank's global open-architecture hedge fund advisory practice, and supervised a team of analysts in the United States, Europe, and Asia. Most recently, Brian was director of hedge fund research for Cantor Advisors LP, the asset management division of Cantor Fitzgerald & Company. He joined Cantor to start up and establish a hedge fund investment practice, and to build and develop an institutional research process and its supporting team.

Atrato Advisors was founded by Brian in October 2008 to meet the rising demand for professional and individualized research, advice, and strategic direction in the alternative investment arena. Atrato is a boutique specializing in hedge fund research and portfolio management advisory services that works with direct allocators to hedge funds as an independent and objective provider of research, risk management, and portfolio advisory services.

Brian believes that although there are many backgrounds that are appropriate and relevant for those wishing to do hedge fund research, one's prior experience should have some relevant strengths in the various aspects of due diligence. Prior experience in trading, investment research, accounting, operations, journalism, quantitative analysis, and risk management are all background jobs that Brian finds complementary to hedge fund due diligence. He points out that the ability to be versatile across all of these areas is a positive for someone wishing to do hedge fund due diligence as a career.

This leads to Brian's advice for anyone considering hedge fund due diligence: Become a good "all-around athlete." There are quantitative, qualitative, investigative, and instinctual skills that one needs to have to be a good analyst. The ability to communicate and craft well-thought-out arguments to invest or not to invest is also a key aspect of the position. Brian believes that if you're good or excel at one thing, you should work on getting stronger in other areas where you are not as experienced.

Brian says that he enjoys the challenge of trying to find the one piece or several pieces of information that are ultimately going to drive his investment decision the most. In nearly all cases, in doing fund research, the client is sitting across the table from a manager who is trying to paint the prettiest possible picture, and it's always in the portfolio manager's best interest to highlight the positives and downplay negatives. Brian looks forward to probing around each aspect of the organization, not knowing where he's going to find that crucial and possibly hidden data point.

The time Brian spends on due diligence for a hedge fund varies greatly, but on average it takes about three to four months. The biggest lesson Brian has learned is to share information with peers and competitors. He thinks it is virtually impossible to know *everything* about a fund manager or his business. There are lots of smart, talented researchers out there who may take a different perspective or focus on different factors than he does, and that's who he wants to communicate with. He feels that if sharing information with a competitor can help protect their client by bringing to their attention a relevant piece of information, then he is acting in the best possible fiduciary manner.

When watching out for a shady manager, Brian points out that there are the usual obvious signs such as questionable business structures, obscure service provider relationships, and evasiveness in the due diligence process. Brian believes that some of the more subtle things are important to look out, for such as risk-taking behavior and tendencies. Identifying patterns of behavior either in trading record or career progression is a softer way of trying to figure out what a portfolio manager is most likely to do when his back is against the wall. As part of their operational due diligence, Atrato also verifies the existence and roles of the specific board members through onshore and offshore counsel.

Brian finds that trustworthy managers always have the most transparency. The more a manager is willing to show an investor (and to help with the verification of his veracity), the better. Although it may sound counterintuitive, Brian points out that bad performance can actually be a sign of honest management. If an investor has good information about a fund's exposures and portfolio holdings, it's usually pretty easy to predict how that manager would have performed in the past. If, based on an analysis of a fund manager's portfolio, you would expect him to do poorly during a certain time period and he actually *didn't*, then a red flag should go up.

Brian doesn't believe in administering a boilerplate DDQ. He finds that using such questionnaires greatly limits the creativity one needs to carefully and effectively analyze an investment opportunity, and it allows the fund manager to predict and carefully massage crafted messages. Most managers produce a similarly formatted Alternative Investment Management Association (AIMA) type questionnaire anyway. The AIMA standard questionnaire is already the most used tool throughout the industry. More candid answers are generated throughout the dialogue with a manager when the conversation is less structured and more free-flowing. A competent and experienced CFO and COO also help the process flow more smoothly.

On the operational side, getting the right infrastructure and service providers and internal operational staff is the key to early success. This also means the manager is investing in his fund early on, but he'll raise money quickly and generally be rewarded in the long run. Brian points out that most hedge fund managers are hardworking, smart people who are trying to do right by their investors.

As a case study, Brian gave us the facts on a 2002 interview with a fund manager who traded a discretionary global macro strategy. The fund manager had pedigree from one of the largest multistrategy hedge funds in the world at the time, and was allowed to show his track record going back to the mid-1990s for profit and loss (P&L) that he managed while employed at his previous firm. There was one notable omission from his track record, as he did not post a performance number for August and September 1998. Of course, this was a crucial stress test for a hedge fund manager, particularly trading a macro strategy, as this was the time of the Russia default and the LTCM collapse. When pressed on this, he claimed that he had closed all his positions prior to August and had coincidentally "sat out" those crucial months. Unsatisfied, Brian pressed further in complete disbelief of this assertion. The portfolio manager became enraged and stormed out of the meeting. Brian states, "I'll never know if he was telling the truth or not, but the fury by which he ended the meeting (something I had never seen before nor have I seen again) was enough to paint a picture of a highly volatile persona and one whom I didn't want managing our money."

Obviously, Brian and Scott have a different approach to hedge fund due diligence. The most notable difference is the use of a standardized DDQ versus the aversion to one. Brian and Scott are both of the opinion that verifying the validity of the board of directors of each fund is of the utmost importance, and that a telltale sign of a good manager is being transparent and forthright with information about himself, his fund, and his background. They both also stress that the real due diligence comes from the interviews and information received, however that information is collected.

RICHARD WILSON, HEDGE FUND GROUP, CHP DESIGNATION, HEDGEFUNDBLOGGER.COM

For this chapter's final interview, Gregory Schink interviewed Richard Wilson about his experience in the hedge fund world and his experience and advice concerning hedge fund due diligence. Richard has a background in capital raising and risk management. He holds a bachelor's degree in business administration from Oregon State University and an MBA in marketing from the University of Portland. Directly out of college, he helped raise capital for an investment bank and a start-up tech firm and then went into risk management consulting and process design advisory work. While he feels that the consulting gave him a unique perspective, he missed the challenge and marketing aspect of raising capital.

Richard moved back into a capital-raising role as a third party marketer for hedge funds, funds of hedge funds, and large asset optimization shops. This position allowed him to help roll out new products and raise capital for existing portfolios. Richard eventually was able to help raise over $225 million in this first third party marketing role and has helped raise another $100 million-plus since. While Richard didn't see as many fund managers each year as an institutional investor may, he received several inquiries each day and quickly learned why investors must cut most managers out of the running, based simply on objective criteria such as assets under management (AUM); there is just not enough time to really look into every manager who comes toward you with a pitch book and one-pager. Richard's most recent role has been running the Hedge Fund Group, CHP Designation, Hedge-FundBlogger.com, and working on related capital-raising training programs, directories, and resources for fund managers.

Our interview went on to probe into what Richard thought were some of the biggest problems in hedge fund due diligence as well as what he thought was useful advice for this field. Poor marketing materials are one of the things that stand out right away to Richard as an area that could use improvement. He believes that many managers with less than $1 billion in AUM have poor marketing systems, sales pipeline development processes, investor relationship management tools, and educational materials. Most professionals who start hedge funds are experts at their domains of trading and portfolio management but have close to no experience in marketing, sales, and capital raising. This can give the wrong message to investors while they complete their due diligence. Richard warned that if the principal of the fund hasn't been coached, if the marketing materials don't clearly articulate the investment process, and if the team doesn't have resources in place to manage the ongoing relationship, it can end the due diligence process or even prevent it from ever starting.

Due diligence calls are another area of improvement for hedge fund managers to work on. Completing due diligence calls is an art in itself. Richard thinks that most managers underestimate the importance of what you say and how you say it during these phone calls. Many institutional investors and almost all institutional consultants now have databases where they record and maintain records on every manager they speak to across the company. If you blow one single phone call with a consultant who advises $500 billion in assets, it could take three to four more phone calls to calm their fears about one issue which could have been misinterpreted in the last phone call you had with them.

Richard's tips for avoiding pain in this area would be to work on possible answers to questions ahead of time and determine how you will reply to important questions regarding portfolio position sizes, risk management, your investment process, and so on. Coordinating who will speak over the phone, practicing your lines, becoming comfortable explaining your investment perspective verbally, and thinking about all of the different ways your words can be interpreted are key aspects of being prepared for a phone interview. If you say something like, "In this market, position sizes mean nothing," that can be taken to mean that you don't keep a consistent position size through varying markets or that you are taking a large amount of risk in the portfolio. Richard warns that everything you say can have two to three meanings and that you should make sure you control that and clarify the meaning for yourself or after others have spoken on your team.

Richard believes organization is another area that is often overlooked by hedge fund managers when it comes to due diligence—having everything ready to send to potential investors before they ask for compliance reports, positions, holdings, sample portfolio weights, historic team adjustments, full bios on team members, audit reports, and the necessary legal documents. Richard warns not to wait until a family office decides not to invest in your firm because you can't produce one of these reports. Be highly organized and efficient when it comes to marketing and you will come off as having been proactive in managing risk, wise in your choice of service providers, and professional in running your business.

Richard always try to advise funds on building their own internal marketing resources because no third-party marketer will ever care more than the actual manager about raising capital for his own fund. Richard thinks it is smart to use third-party marketing services in the appropriate circumstances but that it shouldn't be the resource that a hedge fund bets its business on. Managers must raise capital on their own as well and move up the learning curve on what it takes to manage a third-party marketer.

Richard also went on to explain some of the most useful tips he commonly sees in hedge fund due diligence. Richard notes that the very best funds have preparation and constant improvement. These funds are always aware of who is going to talk, what will be covered, and what could be improved before and after each due diligence phone call that occurs. These can be intense and lengthy calls, and it will help improve your performance if you take notes on what is said during the call or ask the consultants for permission to record them for later review.

Questions will be asked that are specific to each fund's performance and background. The answers to these are very important, such as explaining the fund's quarter 3 (Q3) performance back in 2006, or why its position size changed from 2007 to 2008, or why the chief investment officer left the firm after five years of running the portfolio. These questions must be answered carefully, yet a manager does not want to bring up all these issues in the PowerPoint presentation or it would be more than 100 pages long. The solution that Richard has found works best is typing up specific answers in one- to three-page Word documents that are complete, accurate, and detailed responses to these tough questions that due diligence will uncover regarding the specific fund and personnel. This allows the manager to either read from the typed responses over the phone or e-mail the consultant the one-page explanation regarding that topic, allowing professionals to review the detailed answer and evidence and then ask any follow-up questions that may arise. This strategy helps the manager demonstrate that he is well organized, prepared, and knowledgeable about the perceived risks of his fund.

Having a lot of clarity is also key. Richard advises managers to know the five points they really want to drive home during the due diligence process about their specific fund. How are you positioning your fund and in what tangible ways is your fund different? Simply saying that your returns are uncorrelated with the stock market and you can make money in any market condition is not tangible or unique but heard every hour in the industry.

Richard has completed due diligence on hundreds of hedge fund managers from the perspective of a marketer but never as an analyst or fund of funds due diligence professional. Typically throughout the industry, though, he thinks the worst type of due diligence process is one that not only uses an AUM figure as a first-pass cutting tool but then also skips through most of the other steps needed to allocate funds. This practice is rampant and bad for investors, bad for the industry, and bad for small, innovative hedge fund managers. It slows down the natural process of evolution in the industry and provides the largest of investors with less appealing long-term returns. The best due diligence Richard has seen is by firms that take on a very limited set of clients each year so they can dedicate adequate resources toward each fund they analyze. It takes time to look at portfolio returns and DDQs, complete on-site visits, and check Web databases on performance. Richard feels that the biggest difference between those who do due diligence right and those who do it wrong are poor talent and resources compared to great experience combined with consistent, detailed-oriented process-driven approaches.

DUE DILIGENCE EFFECTS ON HEDGE FUNDS

To understand due diligence and how it affects a hedge fund, one must look into what can happen when due diligence is lacking or not up to par. Let's examine three infamous examples of hedge funds blowing up and point out some examples of how good due diligence could have protected investors from mistake and/or fraud. The examples used here are Long Term Capital Management, Bayou Hedge Fund, and Bernie Madoff Investment Securities.

Long Term Capital Mangement

Long Term Capital Management (LTCM) was a U.S. hedge fund founded in 1994 by John Meriwether, the former vice chairman and head of bond trading at Salomon Brothers. The fund's trading strategies were based upon various arbitrage designs combined with high amounts of leverage. Meriwether approached various business owners, celebrities, and university endowments, but most of the seed money came from companies and individuals connected to the financial industry. When LTCM began trading, the company had amassed just over $1.01 billion in capital.[1]

LTCM used mathematical models to find fixed-income arbitrage opportunities in various government bonds. The managers were making successful trades betting on convergence strategies in these bonds and had amassed annualized returns of over 40 percent in their first few years. As their success grew, so did their assets under management; at the beginning of 1998, the firm had equity of $4.72 billion.

This increasing capital base and unheard-of performance put pressure on LTCM managers to continue to invest the assets they were acquiring, only they had run out of good fixed-income arbitrage plays. LTCM then moved away from the fixed-income arbitrage that had worked so well for it and strayed into merger arbitrage, equity options, interest rate derivatives, and interest rate sweeps.

By the time LTCM had started to invest in the more exotic derivatives, its AUM was $4.72 billion but it had borrowed over $124.5 billion with assets of around $129 billion, for a debt-to-equity ratio of about 25 to 1. LTCM had off-balance-sheet derivative positions with a notional value of approximately $1.25 trillion.

The Russian financial crisis that started in August 1998 triggered a flight from foreign bonds to U.S. treasuries, which destroyed LTCM's

---

[1]Nicholas Dunbar, *Inventing Money: The Story of Long-Term Capital Management and the Legends Behind It* (New York: John Wiley & Sons, 2000).

fixed-income arbitrage play and caused huge losses of over $1.5 billion. This caused investors to move for liquidity in their LTCM positions, and the AUM of LTCM plummeted from $2.3 billion to $400 million in under a month. This translated to a leverage ratio of over 250 to 1 at the end of September 1998. The fund was eventually liquidated by 2000.

LTCM teaches us an important fact about hedge fund due diligence: Know and verify that the hedge fund manager will stay in his designated style. When investing in various hedge funds for diversification across styles, investors are trusting that managers will not stray from their designated styles to chase the money. As LTCM had success and grew larger, its managers felt more pressure to continue to deliver returns greater than 40 percent. As the good fixed-income arbitrage dried up, they moved into derivatives to fill the void and maintain the momentum that investors had come to expect out of the fund. Had LTCM stuck with what it had excelled at from the beginning, fixed-income arbitrage, and realized that every year wasn't going to yield a 40 percent yield, it would have been in much better shape to weather the Russian financial crisis of 1998.

Bayou Hedge Fund Group

Another example of hedge fund due diligence gone bad was the Bayou Hedge Fund Group. This was a conglomerate of companies and hedge funds founded by Samuel Israel III in 1996. The group raised $450 million from investors.

A very simple background check of Mr. Israel would have shown that he had a National Association of Securities Dealers (NASD) membership violation in accordance with Series 55 requirements and was censured and fined $8,500. This should have been a huge red flag, and an easy one to uncover at that. Mr. Israel also claimed that he attended Tulane University, but a simple call to the registrar confirms that he was placed on academic suspension and subsequently left school without receiving a degree. The term *attended* does not mean he received his degree, but the fact that he does not have an undergraduate degree should have raised a warning flag at the very least. Lastly, a criminal background check would have found that Mr. Israel was convicted of a DUI and possession of marijuana at the age of 43. Although a DUI is not necessarily a deal breaker, the fact that he was 43 years old when it happened and was also found to be carrying marijuana at the time is a sign of a poor sense of moral character and judgment. One of these findings alone could easily be dismissed, but the combination of all three indicates a much deeper personality flaw and should have stopped any investor from placing trust with Mr. Israel.

This is a prime example of where hedge fund due diligence had not included a thorough manager background check. Mr. Israel's statements and actual background showed vast discrepancies. A thorough background check compared to the statements Mr. Israel provided would have raised the first red flag. Another red flag would have come up due to some of the events that had occurred in Mr. Israel's life (i.e., the DUI). A hedge fund manager holds a great amount of responsibility and therefore should have displayed virtuous traits throughout his personal and professional life prior to becoming a hedge fund manager.

Bernard L. Madoff Investment Securities

The most prominent example of due diligence gone awry is Bernie Madoff. Madoff's strategy was much more in-depth than the usual fraud, and to understand it, one must understand how he got started and his background.

Madoff founded the firm Bernard L. Madoff Investment Securities LLC in 1960 with money he earned working as a lifeguard and sprinkler installer. The firm specialized in trading penny stocks, and the technology the firm developed eventually became the NASDAQ. The firm began to function as a third market provider, which bypassed exchange specialist firms by directly executing orders over the counter from retail brokers.

Madoff used this function as a way to defer any electronic record of transactions he supposedly was making for his clients. By trading all of his options over the counter, he could give the image that he was bypassing exchange specialist firms and making trades directly through retail brokers, and thereby eliminate any paper trail of those trades.

Although this would make only a savvy investor suspicious of Madoff's trades, one aspect that should have thrown up a red flag from the beginning was clients' lack of electronic access to the accounts. The only proof of their holdings was the paper statements they received monthly in the mail.

There are many highly respected third-party administrators, prime brokers, and audit firms. Madoff had dealings with none of these and was in charge of doing custody, trading, and administration of every investment in his fund. He also turned down the opportunity to have managed accounts with clients, even to the detriment of losing billions of dollars of investments, because of it. This furthered the lack of transparency of his actual underlying investments.

Madoff had actually served as the chairman of the board of directors and on the board of governors of the NASD, and maybe his past credentials had lured more people into his investments.

The part of due diligence that is highlighted by the entire Madoff fraud is transparency, or the lack thereof. Obviously there are in-house trading methods, black-box algorithms, and proprietary secrets that each manager must keep secret to ensure his edge in the hedge fund industry, but electronic documentation of the underlying funds held by the fund does not necessarily give away those strategies. Proper due diligence on Madoff's fund should have raised red flags due to the fact that he was in control of every aspect of the investment process, didn't have a respectable auditor, and would provide no proof of any underlying investment.[2]

In an interesting side note, about half of Madoff's investors were net winners even after his fund blew up, meaning they had earned/withdrawn more than their initial investment.[3]

CHAPTER SUMMARY

This chapter provides information on recent hedge fund due diligence trends as well as two interviews with due diligence experts, one from within a family office and the other at an institutional consulting firm. Some key lessons from this chapter include the following:

- If you are looking to work in the hedge fund due diligence space Scott Freund suggests gaining experience in legal, accounting, and various investment arenas. Brian Reich suggests also being an "all around athlete" in many different disciplines.
- Good due diligence takes a very thorough professional who works on the "trust but verify" basis who takes nothing at face value.
- You can often tell a lot just by how open a hedge fund is to letting you speak to their board of advisers, auditors, prime brokers, or other service providers.
- Due diligence on a hedge fund can sometimes take more than six months but often lasts just two to four months.
- While hedge fund managers are often experts in trading, risk management and portfolio management few are trained in marketing, sales, or managing due diligence processes and this leads to problems.

---

[2]Maureen O'Hara, *Market Microstructure Theory* (Oxford: Blackwell, 1995), 190. ISBN 1-55786-443-8.
[3]Ibid.

REVIEW QUESTIONS

1. This chapter stresses that the main lesson to take away from Long Term Capital Management is that
   a. It is important that a hedge fund manager stay within his designated *style*, or investment mandate scope.
   b. Foreign exchange investing inside of hedge funds can be very risky when those bets are made using only a single prime brokerage firm.
   c. Even well-respected hedge funds can blow up.
2. This chapter indicates that _____ is bad for investors, bad for the industry, and particularly bad for emerging hedge fund managers.
   a. Too much transparency.
   b. Too much compliance reporting.
   c. Eliminating hedge funds from due diligence processes mostly based on AUM.
   d. Eliminating hedge funds from due diligence processes mostly based on background checks.
3. True or false: In this chapter it is suggested that you take every piece of feedback from investors, and each question they ask, and work the detailed answers into your PowerPoint presentation so that you come off as 100 percent prepared and well established to all investors.
4. True or false: It is best to remain highly flexible during hedge fund due diligence calls while presenting your strategy and team—this way your team can adapt on the fly to whoever on the team feels like taking the lead in presenting the details of your investment process and risk management tools to the firm completing the due diligence.
5. Typically, many hedge fund managers _____ how important hedge fund due diligence calls are with potential investors.
   a. Underestimate
   b. Overestimate
6. True or false: Hedge fund due diligence takes in-depth quantitative and qualitative analysis skills to figure out what is missing or is not being said, and some of this comes with experience.
7. Brian Reich has found that _____ managers have the most transparency.
   a. Small hedge fund.
   b. Large hedge fund.
   c. Trustworthy.
   d. Fast-growing.
8. Which of the following is *not* suggested as a way to identify potential problems that exist within the hedge fund during a due diligence process?

a. Evasive behavior.
b. Questionable business structures.
c. Small portfolio management teams.
d. Obscure service provider relationships.

9. According to the interviews in this chapter, the hedge fund due diligence process takes _____ months to be completed.
a. 2 to 4
b. 8 to 12
c. 18 to 24
d. 4 to 12

10. True or false: Hedge fund due diligence professionals always use boiler-plate due diligence questionnaires, so once you have completed one of these you will be able to simply use that for all future inquiries.

Answers: To view the answers to these questions, please see http://dHedgeFundTraining.com/Answers

CHAPTER **7**

Giant Hedge Funds

On the mountains of truth you can never climb in vain: Either you will reach a point higher up today, or you will be training your powers so that you will be able to climb higher tomorrow.
— Friedrich Nietzsche

While most hedge funds are small in size it is typically the largest of hedge funds which are most secretive. These hedge funds have assets, secrets, and processes to protect from hungry competitors. This chapter provides a unique insight to some of the marketing, operational, and investing best practices of hedge funds with $1 billion or more in assets under management.

Why important: If you are trying to grow a hedge fund it can help to see what the hedge funds who are receiving most of the new incoming capital are doing. In this chapter we provide some clues and a peek behind the curtain to what the largest of hedge funds are doing different from smaller fund managers in the industry.

BEST PRACTICES FROM $1 BILLION-PLUS HEDGE FUNDS

Following is a list of ten best practices that I have seen $1 billion-plus hedge funds employing that are more often than not missing within small teams of hedge fund professionals. Large well run hedge funds often have:

1. *Better research processes* in place, and these are constantly being improved in many ways every quarter. They focus on Kazien—constant improvement.

2. *Documentation.* Their compliance processes, operational procedures, compliance checks, internal controls, hiring processes, and risk management techniques are all documented in great detail to help ensure consistent quality and improve what is being carried out.

3. *International marketing and sales teams* which cover institutional investors and consultants in at least Europe and the United States if not also in Australia, South Africa, South America, and Asia.

4. *Deep pedigree.* With larger pocketbooks, the largest of hedge funds are able to retain the most experienced experts not only as adjunct advisers to the fund but full-time employees or consultants who provide daily or weekly insights on upcoming investment opportunities.

5. *Human resources strategies.* Many small hedge funds do not have any long-term talent development, or Star Employee hiring practices in place. Larger hedge funds do and must keep their organization moving forward and growing over the long term.

6. *Master DDQs.* Every large hedge fund I know of has a very thorough master due diligence questionnaire that is constantly updated. The larger the hedge fund the more likely it is that their investors will be asking for a very thorough DDQ during the due diligence phase.

7. *Superior marketing.* Larger hedge funds have moved to the top of the learning curve when it comes to figuring out how to raise capital. They use multi-modality marketing channels and materials and they have relationship development processes and goals in place which match up with the long-term growth goals of the fund. They are also more than willing to invest in the best graphic designers and sales copy writers who can provide another edge over those who skimp on their image and marketing presence.

8. *More in-house functions.* While large hedge funds still use service providers and rely upon business partners many of them have large enough staffs and unique enough processes that some work such as some investment research, operations, accounting, or marketing may be done in-house instead of being outsourced to service providers such as administrators or third party marketers.

9. *More verification points.* The largest of hedge funds have been asked 500 times for their holdings, and 3,000 times for their PowerPoint presentation. They have completed hundreds of due diligence processes and are use to working with consultants who need to check every fact, assertion, and claim. They are used to operating within the world of providing evidence for everything said, and because of this may quickly meet the requests of investors who ask for such evidence.

10. *Long-term strategies and goals.* Most large hedge funds I know of plan for the next three to five or five to seven years strategically in who they

hire, market their fund to, and where they open offices. In contrast most smaller hedge funds are very focused on day-to-day or month-to-month operations and most think in terms of one- to three-year plans. When investors see the fund planning for investing in the long haul, it shows, and that is part of why some larger hedge funds receive more allocations than small ones. They have the infrastructure and mind-set more in common with an institutional investor.

RICHARD ZAHM, PORTFOLIO MANAGER, SECOND ANGEL FUND

Our first interview in this chapter is with Richard Zahm, portfolio manager of Second Angel Fund.

Richard Wilson: What type of hedge fund do you work for?

Richard Zahm: I've focused on asset-based lending (ABL) funds, specifically bridge lending funds that provide short-term financing secured by commercial real estate.

Richard Wilson: Can you explain how that strategy relates to a more typical long/short equity fund?

Richard Zahm: The strategies have all of the attributes that equity funds are now faced with: transparency, compliance, coordination of lock periods with specific investments/loans. Fund sizes range from start-ups to around $800 million. I've served as co-founder, portfolio manager, underwriter, servicer, and CCO. The unique element of this type of investment is that it crosses several disciplines and regulatory regimes: real estate, lending, and investing; state regulations with multiple agencies in each state, as well as a federal overlay. The segment was noncorrelated, but now finds itself subject to the backlash brought about by unrelated residential mortgages and the credit crunch.

Richard Wilson: It sounds like you have worked in a variety of roles, including both small funds and an $800 million fund. What would you say is the number one difference between your hedge fund operations in the $800 million fund and that of a sub–$100 million hedge fund firm? What really makes your firm stand out in terms of operations, trading, or risk management?

Richard Zahm: A smaller ABL fund contains fewer assets and, as a result, there's tighter focus by senior management as to what's contained in the portfolio. Personal contact with borrowers and investors is greater and there's a good sense of the details of each specific position. It's a lot like being in a small boat: You're aware of subtle shifts in everything around you.

You're also more exposed to changes in conditions than you are in a larger vessel. A bigger fund provides more opportunity to diversify risk across a greater number of investments. Performing loans in the fund provide a cushion against delinquencies and defaults—that is, so long as the diversification model was maintained. However, there's a strong tendency for managers to follow a cookie-cutter approach, replicating previous successful loans in terms of type, size, and location. The thinking is, "It worked before, it'll work again." Although this approach solves the immediate challenge of deploying additional investment dollars flowing into a fund, it actually works *against* the core strategy of diversifying loans in a fund. Concentrations begin to appear. Portfolios become lumpy, either by loan type or, worse, by loan size. As investment funds get larger, it becomes increasingly difficult to maintain lender discipline.

Richard Wilson: How can funds like yours fight against this?

Richard Zahm: The differentiator for us has been a combination of discipline and size itself. We lend on what we know, and keep on top of the loans, the borrowers, and the individual markets.

Richard Wilson: What advice would you offer to small to medium-size hedge fund managers who have yet to bridge the gap between the $5 to $100 million mark and the $1 billion-plus mark?

Richard Zahm: Focus on the additional requirements that larger institutional investors have, while maintaining the practices that enable you to succeed at a smaller size.

Richard Wilson: That's a great piece of advice. I think many times managers are hesitant to make large changes to their processes if they feel like it is going to slow them down or get in the way of how they have operated successfully in the past. Do you have an example of this?

Richard Zahm: Compliance and due diligence material and documentation might not seem relevant early on, but having the processes in place that can prove performance are the costs of admission as the fund grows. It's a heavy burden for a small fund and it won't always be attributable to operations, but keep with it.

Richard Wilson: Great, thanks for that suggestion. This is valuable to just about every emerging manager right now who is planning to keep up with further regulatory developments.

From the perspective of working in a very large hedge fund, what do small hedge funds not realize, which you could share as a lesson, tip, or strategy that would help them secure far more investments from institutional investors than they may be receiving now?

Richard Zahm: From the start, identify which institutional lenders are even in a position to invest in small funds. Many are proscribed from investing in funds below a certain size, or in making investments smaller than a given amount that could represent too large a position in a fund. From there, determine if there is a familiarity with the strategy the fund is using and how there might be a fit.

Richard Wilson: I think that hits on a very common frustration in the industry: that smaller funds cannot become larger because most of the capital is being sent to the funds that are already above a certain threshold, such as $100 million. Any other advice in regard to marketing to institutional investors?

Richard Zahm: Yes, also recognize the very, very slow pace that many institutional investors often have. They're under constraints themselves. Provide information to them in the format they want.

Richard Wilson: Great. I think this is overlooked, and many managers can spoil a potential partnership by checking in every three days regarding progress or status of a potential allocation or due diligence questionnaire (DDQ) process. In my experience, the sales cycle for a large institutional investor is 12 to 16 months or more. You will be sending the wrong signals and moving away from having a solid relationship with the potential investor if you are a pest.

What group of institutional investors do you see as having a very strong long-term interest in hedge funds, and where do you see some slack in demand in terms of allocations to hedge funds over the next 5 to 10 years?

Richard Zahm: ABL funds will continue to attract investors seeking steady, uncorrelated returns using a simple, transparent model. They will be appealing to more patient money allocations, taking on more of a hybrid private equity (PE)/hedge fund structure.

Richard Wilson: So you believe that unique, transparent, simple models will grow in assets much more quickly than competitors who work in a more complex or black-box type environment?

Richard Zahm: Yes, I do.

Richard Wilson: For those who want to grow to over $1 billion in assets under management (AUM), what are your top five tips for hedge fund managers who have less than $100 million in assets under management but would like to improve the institutional quality of their fund?

Richard Zahm: My advice would be to focus in on:

1. Transparency.
2. Prominence in the industry.

3. Innovation.
4. Consistency.
5. Investor communications.

Richard Wilson: Very valuable—this whole book could be on those five ideas
only and be worth a lot to many fund managers today. We have touched
on transparency in many places in this book; it is more important than
ever. Also, prominence in the industry, or *authority positioning*, as I like
to call it, is something that I speak on but haven't heard many managers
mention. I think that more than 90 percent of hedge funds are started
based on portfolio management and trading expertise and not on capital-
raising or marketing abilities. This leads many hedge funds to be very
detailed in their risk management, trading, and investment processes but
light on public relations, investor databases, investor relationship management, investor communications, and authority positioning. This means
that many of the skills and practices of the manager may go unnoticed.

One last comment to what you just said, the importance of consistency:
Often institutional investors will knock managers off of a short list if their
average holding time, volatility, team, position sizes, liquidity, returns,
investment process, operations, or risk management processes are not
consistent. From their point of view, input hopefully equals output, and
if the input is changed in a completely positive way, it can be seen as an
unknown variable that the investor does not want to take a chance with.
Typically, managers I have worked with only learn of this after losing
some mandates for these types of reasons.

What have you learned *not* to do, or what have you stopped doing
related to trading or operations that was hurting your firm's position as a
high-quality fund management business? Any lessons or tips to share on
this point?

Richard Zahm: Tight focus on lending discipline. Constantly relate local
market conditions to macro elements. Closely monitor related segments:
local and regional institutional lenders.

Richard Wilson: I think this is related to consistency once again, consistently performing those activities to stay on target. Besides AUM, what
do you believe is most important for a hedge fund to focus on improving
when thinking about institutionalizing a hedge fund? Risk management?
Trading processes? Research? Pedigree?

Richard Zahm: In the end, it all comes down to consistent performance over
the long term. Other elements will be listed as being critical, and they
should be addressed. But in the end it all comes down to doing what you
say you're going to do, and being responsive to investors.

Richard Wilson: How has your firm gotten past the "under $100 million, no institutional-quality operations" objection in the past? Gone to smaller investors who don't hold this objection? Met with investors face-to-face? Any lessons learned here?

Richard Zahm: Institutional quality has been less of an issue. Size is the hurdle. Small investors have a number of advantages. They're loyal, they listen, and, most important, they're only answering to themselves. Redemption requests are linked to the performance of the fund, not the underperformance of other funds. Smaller investors wanting full redemption, for example, don't have the same impact as large investors wanting to cash out all at once.

Richard Wilson: What are the top three resources or tools that you use to run your hedge fund that are worth more than anything else? What are the most valuable resources that you could recommend to others?

Richard Zahm: The network of bankers, attorneys, brokers, and other fund managers provide the most critical tools. The network provides deal flow, and it also provides a window to what's happening outside of the immediate loan and investment opportunities. Properly used, it also supplies a backstop on assumptions, something that can become distorted in the focus on details.

Richard Wilson: How important do you think service providers are to the success of your fund? What process have you used to select these service providers and what lessons have you learned about working with both large and small service providers that your firm has worked with? You do not have to use any names of individual firms—generic advice is fine.

Richard Zahm: Service providers have traditionally played a minor, ancillary role in our segment due to the simplicity of our model and the transparency of operations. Because of the relatively low velocity of individual investments, quarterly investor letters and annual audits have been sufficient.

Richard Wilson: In other sections of this book, many fund managers have talked about how important service providers are to their fund. Can you explain your perspective further?

Richard Zahm: Size of service providers is less important than their familiarity with our industry segment. Size, in fact, actually worked against us: Inferior services were provided at higher cost. In exchange for working with a provider with broad name recognition, we were saddled with less skilled junior personnel. We ended up teaching *them* our business, while paying for the privilege.

Richard Wilson: That's a great case study example of the downside of working with the largest of service providers. I have experienced this same trouble while working with very large service providers. I think there is a difference between a service provider with niche knowledge and an experienced team versus a giant of a firm that hires 100 new professionals each year. So you would suggest that really examining the team of the service provider is key?

Richard Zahm: Sorting out the claims of proficiency versus actual capability is key.

Richard Wilson: Do you have any other pieces of advice related to operational hedge fund best practices that you could share with other managers in the industry?

Richard Zahm: Always keep in mind that you're a small business. Even if the AUM is enormous, basic start-up considerations remain.

Richard Wilson: Great advice—at least a third of the questions I get relate to running a small business as a hedge fund manager. Many times hedge funds aren't described or analyzed as small businesses but they are in fact just that.

What is the most challenging aspect of week-to-week or month-to-month operations? How has your firm adapted to this challenge? What tools have you found that help you manage this?

Richard Zahm: We've gone from a dependable, steady-state environment to one that's witnessing a dramatic loss of equity over a short period of time.

Richard Wilson: What specific changes has that brought to how you operate?

Richard Zahm: Investment models that have stood the test of time have been put into question and are demanding new approaches and the incorporation of skills that were earlier separate.

Richard Wilson: Can you give us an example?

Richard Zahm: Bridge lending, mezzanine lending, and equity investment are now intermingled with workouts, turnarounds, and development. Models that were geared to go forward are grinding in reverse, and we have to contend not only with market changes but with the new role being played by the government, all while the larger fund regulation model is being modified. We're in the crosshairs of regulators coming to grips not just with mortgage lending but with banking and investor relations.

The tools are pretty straightforward. It comes down to obtaining and processing information, information that ranges from market to regulatory, local to macro. It's sophisticated, and changes come on what seem to be a daily basis. That said, the opportunities are enormous for those with the right combination of talent, expertise, and investment.

Richard Wilson: Thank you for all of this valuable information provided here today—we appreciate your time invested here.

Richard Zahm: No problem, thank you.

SCOTT COHEN, PRESIDENT AND CEO, HEDGE SOLUTIONS

Our next short interview is with Scott Cohen, president and CEO of Hedge Solutions, a Los Angeles–based fund administrator that also offers back-office consulting services to small and large hedge funds. Scott has worked with numerous hedge fund managers over his career and has seen firsthand funds grow quickly, stagnate, and even close down. Over time he has picked up some trends, best practices, and lessons to share with managers in the industry.

Richard Wilson: What operational best practices do you see hedge funds picking up that are somewhat new to the industry as a whole but have existed in the largest of hedge funds for some time?

Scott Cohen: In light of recent fraud activity in the industry and the desire for greater oversight by the federal government, fund managers are starting to adapt by addressing a greater need for transparency. The tone at the top is still as important as ever, as it is ultimately up to management to ensure that operations are structured to meet the needs of the marketplace. For example, information sharing through periodic investor communications, such as newsletters and investor web sites, allows hedge funds to provide some background on fund performance. Additionally, investor web sites allow investors real-time and convenient access to account information; not only can an investor access his capital balance but also current news, audit reports, and K-1s. Some fund managers hold routine conference calls to update clients, which also provide an opportunity for investors to ask questions. Performance statistics and attribution analysis posted on the web site are shared by managers with their investors on an ongoing basis.

Richard Wilson: The one piece I picked out there that is not often put into practice is the routine conference calls with investors. Most hedge funds I have met with less than $250 million in assets do not host these calls, and instead handle all communications on an individual basis. I think that offering such transparency to the team and chief investment officer is a good way to keep the lines of communication open in both directions.

Based on the best practices of $1 billion-plus hedge funds and fast-growing hedge funds, where do you believe most fund managers should be reinvesting their money?

Scott Cohen: Hedge funds should be directing their efforts and resources toward capturing and reporting information that is meaningful to their investors, while also being mindful of the current and potential regulatory requirements of the investment adviser. Middle- and back-office operations, though essential to the overall effectiveness of the organization, are often overlooked. Most hedge funds use third-party administrators and rely on them to accurately report the financial results of the fund and each partner. By shadowing the administrator, the hedge fund will be able to provide added review on the administrator and any reporting issues can be addressed effectively.

Richard Wilson: What best practices do you see $1 billion-plus hedge funds implementing that almost all small hedge funds ignore or discount?

Scott Cohen: Every hedge fund needs to consider internal controls and regulatory compliance. Funds smaller than $1 billion don't always consider instituting proper compliance programs, but compliance is ever more critical in today's environment. Regulatory bodies expect fund managers to implement and monitor their compliance effectively. Moreover, institutional investors now expect fund managers to have formal compliance programs and strict internal controls, yet this is one area that small funds ignore as they continue to target smaller clients that may lack institutional investors. With the industry evolving toward stricter regulation, one way for smaller funds to achieve a competitive advantage is to implement stricter compliance mechanisms such as leveraging the use of their current administrator or using an outsourced compliance service.

Richard Wilson: Almost every hedge fund manager I know would like to become a $1 billion-plus fund, for obvious reasons. Where should these managers now invest money if they are already growing quickly and gaining assets rapidly?

Scott Cohen: Hedge fund managers who are experiencing quick growth are obviously aware of the need to gain better information in order to achieve alpha. However, they are not always aware of the importance of ensuring operational needs such as internal trade reconciliation with the broker and adequate record keeping. As the investment adviser grows, middle- and back-office requirements also expand. Hedge fund managers need to be certain that internal compliance programs are robust enough to integrate shifting staff roles and growth due to new hires. Along the same lines, portfolio risk systems and back-office systems must be implemented so as to manage the company's business risk.

Richard Wilson: Where do you see hedge funds slowing down their own growth due to lack of resources or skills? What mistakes do you see being made by very fast-growing $100 million-plus funds?

Scott Cohen: Very fast-growing $100 million-plus funds experience problems when they deviate from their principles on the portfolio. As management of the portfolio shifts from one investment strategy to another in order to make up the losses incurred in the portfolio, the potential for further losses occurs. More often than not, over the long term, a minor enhancement to the original investment strategy yields better results than abandoning it. Another area of difficulty is lack of objectivity and proper due diligence in the investment made. This could be caused in part by lack of requisite skills. Sometimes investors will fully redeem from a particular fund if they perceive that the fund manager is not addressing their needs from a reporting perspective or not communicating effectively.

Richard Wilson: True. I also believe that a risk just as dangerous as poor performance is coming across as inconsistent over time. If you have changed your investment process once or twice, what may stop you from changing it again? If you produced returns with one set of tools through up and down markets, can we really trust that you can do the same now with a larger team, and a so-called upgraded investment process?

 BONUS VIDEO MODULE

To watch a video on the importance of investment research versus investment processes, please type this URL into your Web browser: http://HedgeFundTraining.com/Research

CHAPTER SUMMARY

This chapter provides some lessons and direct insights from how large $1 billion-plus hedge funds are operated. Some key lessons from this chapter include the following:

- Small hedge funds have a more granular feel of individual positions, while larger funds make more strategic long-term decisions and have a different focus.
- Larger funds are typically able to diversify investments across a larger pool of assets, especially within hard asset and large capital requirement areas.
- Many large hedge fund managers have learned to keep their diversity model in place the hard way. It is tempting to run with what seems to be working instead of diversifying your investments.

- Strong internal controls, compliance procedures, and risk reporting are things that large hedge funds have in place that most small hedge funds struggle with.
- It is recommended that to compete with the largest of hedge funds, you should pay attention to investor requirements for large investors without losing sight of what made you a successful small or medium-size hedge fund.
- To help compete against giant hedge funds and emulate their success, Richard Zahm suggests focusing on transparency, prominence within the industry, innovation, consistency, and investor communications.

REVIEW QUESTIONS

1. True or false: Scott Cohen states in this chapter that he doesn't believe that the "tone at the top" is important any longer as financial controls and compliance processes have taken the front stage within the hedge fund industry.
2. True or false: A risk just as big as poor performance is appearing and acting inconsistent over time.
3. Richard Zahm suggests that even when you are managing $800 million or $1 billion, _____ still apply.
   a. Business negotiation tactics.
   b. Business start-up considerations.
   c. Capital-raising best practices.
4. A lesson to take away from large hedge fund operations is that the size of a hedge fund service provider does not always determine the quality of service; the most important thing to consider is _____.
   a. How they work with other service providers.
   b. How familiar they are with your strategy.
   c. How many years they have been in business.
   d. How familiar they are already with your team.
5. In this chapter it is suggested that the advantages of building a large $1 billion fund based on smaller investors include all of the following except:
   a. Loyalty.
   b. They listen.
   c. They are only answering to themselves.
   d. They complete due diligence more quickly.
6. True or false: To stay in the forefront of the mind of potential investors, it is a best practice of very large hedge funds to check in on the status of due diligence processes every three to four days.

7. True or false: In this chapter it is suggested that you forget about being an authority on your subject and your prominence in the industry, and focus instead on having high-quality financial controls, infrastructure, and institutional-quality operations in place.

   Answers: To view the answers to these questions, please see http://HedgeFundTraining.com/Answers

CHAPTER 8

Governance Best Practices

*Excellence is an art won by training and habituation. We do not
act rightly because we have virtue or excellence, but we rather
have those because we have acted rightly. We are what we
repeatedly do. Excellence, then, is not an act but a habit.*

—Aristotle

T his chapter provides an interview-based overview of fund governance and
the ways in which many hedge funds are creating more robust checks and
balances in their own fund operations to prevent abuse and create a more
sustainable business at the same time.

Why important: Fund governance is by far the most consistently ignored
part of running a hedge fund as a real business. Every year the importance of
having strong governance procedures in place grows, and we see no slowing
down or potential reversal of this trend.

 BONUS VIDEO MODULE

To watch a video on hedge fund governance best practices and
practical strategies, please type this URL into your Web browser:
http://HedgeFundTraining.com/Governance

Fund governance is a valuable area to learn more about because most
funds have relatively weak internal controls, independent boards, and checks
and balance systems in place. Most funds are focused first on managing their

portfolio and second on raising capital; operational issues or governance procedures are often afterthoughts or formalities.

Lately the hedge fund industry has been marred by cases of fraud. In some cases individual employees of a hedge fund committed acts which placed the hedge fund manager's business in jeopardy. If you don't have these governance procedures in place, you may be opening the door for a future employee to commit such acts. No internal control or structure can completely prevent fraud or abuse, but it can help—and it can also show investors that you have reinvested in the stability of your own business.

ANDREW MAIN, MANAGING PARTNER, STRATTON STREET CAPITAL LLP

Our team recently completed an in-depth interview with Andrew Main, managing partner at Stratton Street Capital LLP. Andrew has been a key participant in placing strong corporate governance rules in place since the inception of the funds under management. His team has picked up many best practices and processes which may aide other hedge fund managers or investors who are seeking to better understand this concept.

Richard Wilson: Why have you personally taken such a strong interest in implementing strong corporate governance procedures?

Andrew Main: Lessons of the past two years have shown that strong independent oversight of a hedge fund should be an important step in an investor's due diligence regarding how a fund is run. As the hedge fund community matures, institutional investors will more and more want to see their interests not only aligned with the manager's but also overseen by a strong independent board. In turn, the board may introduce new opportunities to the investment manager or adviser in attracting investors to the fund through their introductions and role in the process.

We are currently living and working through a very dynamic time. As our industry increasingly becomes more institutionalized it moves away from its reliance on a leveraged high net worth (HNW) client investor base. Many funds will have also learned the lesson of relying too heavily on the fund of funds sector but will want to attract institutional capital directly. One of the roles of the fund of funds as the institutional investor's gatekeeper was to act as their eyes and ears on what was actually going on in the fund or in the fund's investment management company. Recent events have shown that in many cases this reliance has not actually been executed. Therefore small boutique funds and managers can easily adopt high corporate governance standards that will put many larger managers to shame. The problem then is how does the institutional investor learn about the manager and his funds?

Richard Wilson: How many board members should there be on a single board?

Andrew Main: Our board has consisted of four to six members at any one time. A diverse board is more valuable than a homogenous one.

Richard Wilson: Can you provide an example of how this has affected potential investors who are completing due diligence on your funds?

Andrew Main: Several years ago we were going through a day's due diligence with a large institutional investor looking to open a managed account with us. It happened to coincide with the quarterly visit from one of the fund's independent board members making his own due diligence review. We therefore suggested the two meet and sit down together and talk alone about us as a manager, in our office. The institutional investor who had spent several hours asking many penetrating questions was lost for words. He openly admitted never having had the opportunity to meet a nonexecutive director of a fund, and said that as a result, he did not know what to ask!

Richard Wilson: Let's start with the basics. What is the purpose of the fund board?

Andrew Main: To collectively be responsible for the central control of the fund by overseeing the affairs of the appropriate interests of the shareholders and relevant stakeholders while at all times ensuring the protection of investors.

Richard Wilson: Can you go into greater detail on exactly what responsibilities the board should hold and what their role is? Maybe something granular enough that hedge fund managers reading this could think about constructing their own board?

Andrew Main: Sure. First off, all directors need to recognize their collective responsibility for the statutory obligations of the fund as well as the strategic, financial, and key personnel matters and focus strongly on the correct delegation, supervision, reporting, monitoring, and control responsibilities of the board. So the first three categories of primary duties are statutory obligations, strategic review, and business and compliance review.

1. Statutory obligations may include such varied matters as:
   a. Preparation of prospectus and constitutional documents; review and approval of annual report and accounts, final dividend, circulars to shareholders, and listing particulars and requirements.

    b. Interim report and accounts and the returns to regulators and stock exchanges.

    c. Compliance with listing rules and their continuing obligations.

    d. Monitoring of marketing activities.

    e. Equal treatment of shareholders.

    f. Accountability to shareholders and responsibility to relevant stakeholders.

2. Strategic review. As part of the exercise, we regard it as best practice to review once a year (we do it at the time of signing off full audited accounts) that the fund, through the execution of its investment policy, has not strayed from its vision and mission as set out in the prospectus. It has a clear vision of its forward-going strategy and future development. It is also a good idea to review where it has come in the past year, especially measured against its peer group.

3. Business and compliance review. As an independent board, it is very important that each board member looks at the fund through a different set of eyes. In an ideal world it is useful to have independent directors who bring fund management, administrative, legal, accounting, and shareholder experience to a fund. It is not necessary for the investment manager or adviser to be on the board, as they may simply attend and report to the board, thus ensuring preservation of independence. However, the board must be able to look at their activities and decide on the appointment and review of the service providers of all functions to the fund.

    This review should include, on an annual basis, the fund company secretary, investment manager, investment adviser, administrator, prime broker, and/or custodian. They should also review the work of the fund auditors, lawyers, and other independent professional advisers such as outside risk monitoring or third-party marketers of the fund. The board should review its annual directors and officers liability insurance to ensure its adequacy to protect all interested parties. It may decide, depending on their complexity, to delegate some of these functions to internal or external committees. The board should also review the overall compliance of the fund to fulfill its functions and that all its statutory duties have been fulfilled.

Richard Wilson: Could you summarize in a more concise way what the high-level duties of board members are?

Andrew Main: Sure. Their primary duties are statutory obligations, strategic and financial matters, key man matters, reporting monitoring and control responsibilities, annual review of composition and effectiveness of the board, and corporate governance.

Richard Wilson: Now, for those who are either sitting on boards or are thinking about improving their board, what types of activities specifically do board members complete each year?

Andrew Main: Well, these activities span across many areas, but here is a bullet-point list of many of the responsibilities our board members take on:

- Development and measuring against the company's vision and mission.
- Strategy of development plan and progress in achieving that plan.
- Significant changes in accounting policy.
- Approval of risk management guidelines.
- Statutory obligations such as monitoring of marketing activities and investor relations procedures.
- Sufficient and timely financial information and reports provided to the board.
- Appointment and review of key service providers such as the prime broker, custodian, administrator, or third-party marketer.
- Ensuring adequate resources are in place for ongoing operations.
- Delegation of board powers to ad hoc committees as needed to address critical issues.
- Ensuring internal controls and procedures are in place and are adequate.
- Obtaining appropriate and timely information to fulfill their obligations.
- Review of all internal and external audit and compliance reports and associated regulatory reviews by third parties.
- Ensuring that a satisfactory compliance regime exists and that all relevant local and international laws, procedures, guidance notes, and controls to combat money laundering, terrorist financing, and other criminal activities are upheld.

Richard Wilson: That seems like more work and implementation than some hedge funds may be willing to do, especially if they are an emerging manager with a new fund.

Andrew Main: In adopting such a structure, it may give the investors comfort that their interests are being protected. The amount and depth of oversight will obviously vary with the development of the fund. It is important not to overload the total expense ratio of the fund with too many wise men but to have sufficient to carry out the basics in the early days of the fund. As the fund matures and we become much more involved in a world dominated by regulatory and investor oversight, the fund needs to demonstrate its strengths to act independently. However, it must not become too bogged down in latest fashions but maintain a standard in the best interest of shareholders and stakeholders.

Richard Wilson: The board oversees many activities. Can you summarize to whom the board members are ultimately responsible?

Andrew Main: The board has ultimate responsibility to the shareholder, relevant stakeholders, their regulator (if regulated), oversight of the outsourced services of the fund, and oversight of the investment manager and the fund.

Richard Wilson: What other advice could you give about properly constructing a board?

Andrew Main: I would suggest, as I mentioned earlier, looking for complementary, diverse skill sets. For example, one of our past boards consisted of a former accountant, a managing director from a bank, an adviser on the topic of corporate governance, and a country adviser specialist. This team was able to help us not only manage our corporate governance but constantly improve it over time as well.

Richard Wilson: Many times when I hear hedge funds discuss corporate governance, the purpose of the board can seem fuzzy, and I believe this may sometimes lead to putting off decisions on forming a board or having a very active board that really oversees the activities of the fund. What would be a concise way to describe the key purpose of the board?

Andrew Main: To collectively be responsible for maximizing the company's success by directing and supervising the affairs of the business and meeting the appropriate interests of the shareholders and relevant stakeholders while enhancing the value of the fund and ensuring protection of investors.

Richard Wilson: Could you provide some guidance on board meetings, how should they be conducted and structured to be effective?

Andrew Main: We hold quarterly meetings and the fund manager/adviser is always present at these meetings. During the meeting we review the fund and its activities, go over the list of shareholders, and conduct corporate governance reviews.

Richard Wilson: In this model some power is taken away from the fund manager and placed with the board members. How do you monitor their participation to ensure they are fulfilling their duties?

Andrew Main: We have the board assess whether members need to be replaced. We allow in-person or over-the-phone participation by board members but expect and have the majority of meetings attended in person.

Richard Wilson: Do you have any closing thoughts before we wrap this up?

Andrew Wilson: A well-functioning board is an excellent trustee and a great resource to all interested parties. Take the time to set up the board the right way and it will work for you over the long term. Make sure and use the board in your due diligence processes.

Richard Wilson: Oftentimes there are references to *nonexecutive advisory* boards or *independent* boards. Can you explain what the term *nonexecutive* really means?

Andrew Main: The majority of board members are the nonexecs. In fact, we do not have any fund managers on our boards. We want the fund managers to report their activity to the board so there can be both integration and independence between the two groups. That further shows the split in roles. We feel that the board members should bring a different view of the fund so we try and have people from different backgrounds—an independent market professional, a lawyer, accountant, administrator, and so on. A nonexecutive does not form part of the executive management of the fund manager or the funds investment decisions but performs a role of central control of the fund through roles of scrutiny, constructive comment on development, ascertaining that risk controls are robust enough and financial data accurate, and so on.

Richard Wilson: I have seen in some of your speeches on governance best practices that you discuss the importance of "board packs." Could you explain what these are exactly?

Andrew Main: A board pack is collated by the fund administrator and is sent out in advance of the meeting to be reviewed by the board of directors. The topics in our last pack were:

- Apologies and appointment of alternates.
- Quorum.
- Directors' interests.
- Minutes of last meeting and any committee meetings (audit, etc.).
- Matters arising.
- Review of financial statements (we reviewed our interims).
- Manager's report.
- Fund manager reviews.
- Marketing review.
- Corporate governance review.
- Annual review of prospectus.
- Administrators' report which includes report of the administrator, compliance review of designated manager and custodian, company's secretary review, stock exchange notices for listing of funds, and continuing obligations.
- Future dates of meetings.
- Any other business.

Richard Wilson: Great, that is helpful. Can you reveal some of the costs associated with building this type of independent board?

Andrew Main: Overall cost of the meetings will be part of the administration cost plus directors' fees and expenses for attending the meeting. I would think you should be looking at $15,000 per annum fees upward per director. Hence, as part of the administration cost, we do review the total expense ratio of the fund, and so on.

DAVID R. KOENIG, CEO OF THE GOVERNANCE FUND, LLC

The second interview we completed for this chapter of the book was with David R. Koenig, CEO of the Governance Fund, LLC, an investment manager which, in their words, "seeks to capture the hidden performance gap between publicly traded companies that are well-governed and those which are poorly governed." I thought this was an interesting strategy, because in studying what good and poor governance mean they would be able to explain some of the importance of having it in place and what that means to investors.

Here is a brief history of David's professional experience: David R. Koenig is the founder and chief executive officer of The Governance Fund, LLC. His work in risk management and governance is internationally recognized. Prior to founding The Governance Fund, LLC, Mr. Koenig served as chair of the board and executive director of the Professional Risk Managers' International Association (PRMIA) and president of the PRMIA Institute. In 2008, he was bestowed PRMIA's top honor, the Higher Standard Award, for his contributions to the global risk profession. He was also named as one of the first 100 members of the Risk Who's Who International Honorary Society, a select group of individuals who have influenced the international practice of risk management.

Richard Wilson: Let's start at the top: Why is strong governance an important thing for both hedge funds and corporations to have in place?

David R. Koenig: The quality of an organization's governance affects its value in three main ways. First, well-governed organizations make better decisions, which leads to expectations of better growth. Second, well-governed firms have imbedded resilience and the ability to change as conditions in an industry or asset class change. Witness the many high-profile, abrupt endings to financial service companies during the 2007–2009 financial crisis. Well-governed companies are resilient, ductile, and complex adaptive systems. In response to stresses, they bend, but don't break. Their strength provides them the opportunity to adjust to new realities. They reform and they remain strong.

Third, investors will more greatly discount their expectations of future earnings for poorly governed companies because they represent a higher risk of surprises. Work in psychology and behavioral finance has shown that people have a strong drive for loss avoidance. They fear large losses much more than they value large gains. In fact, the dislike of large losses has been valued at more than two times the desire for gains. So companies that present investors with the possibility of large losses are assigned higher discount rates by the investors. As noted earlier, poorly governed companies are more likely to be subject to large, surprise losses. In some cases, those surprise losses will end their existence. Well-governed companies, however, can come to be perceived as presenting a lower risk of large, surprise losses, and their value increases due to their lower discount factor applied to their future earnings.

Richard Wilson: So basically, having strong governance in place helps the organization avoid pitfalls and avoid closing down due to operational business missteps as well?

David R. Koenig: In short, good governance adds value; poor governance detracts from it.

Richard Wilson: Can you provide us with some governance factors you look at in corporations that could also be assessed by investors looking at hedge fund governance structures?

David R. Koenig: Sure. From a structural standpoint, some of these factors include:

- Chairman/CEO separation.
- Board composition.
- Office turnover.
- Late filings.
- Change in external auditing.
- Shareholder controls.

From an accounting and forensics standpoint—in other words, how companies "live" their governance—some factors include:

- Accrued expenses.
- Deferred taxes.
- Late filings.
- Extraordinary expenses.
- Actuarial assumptions related to pension liabilities.

Richard Wilson: While governance is something that most fund managers agree is important to have in place, how come more hedge fund managers do not already have these practices in place?

David R. Koenig: The difference may stem from whether you view your company as a business, or just a trading strategy. If the former, you have a very different perspective on your relationship to your customers. Good governance happens when the process of decision making and implementation is accountable, transparent, responsive, effective, and efficient. It doesn't happen by accident—it only works when it is a priority and it is intentional. You have such an intention when you focus on the needs of your customers first.

Richard Wilson: Everyone in the hedge fund industry talks about the need for "increased transparency," but beside the use of separate accounts, what types of processes or access can hedge fund managers provide investors to increase their level of transparency?

David R. Koenig: Clients have a right to understand what is being done with their funds, both in terms of the strategies being pursued and the risks being taken. Without transparency to positions and trades, it is difficult for investors to have complete confidence that their investment mandate is being adhered to, or that their expectations are being met. Therefore, transparency of all positions and trades taken by The Governance Fund, LLC, on behalf of a client is available via two methods designed to protect the proprietary nature of the process we use.

Investors who are willing to sign a nondisclosure agreement with an intellectual property clause related to the reverse-engineering of strategies can have complete transparency with respect to all positions and all transactions on a daily basis. Alternatively, without any additional agreements, all investors in the funds that we manage are given full transparency on all positions and all trades, five times per year, on any day they choose. Using these methods, we as the investment manager provide investors in the fund with the appropriate transparency to our operations.

In addition to these two views into the positions, we have created a Governance and Risk Management Advisory Board, composed of internationally recognized leaders in risk management, governance, and finance. They meet quarterly to review the risk management and governance of The Governance Fund, LLC, and the minutes of their meeting related to this review are made available to all investors in the funds that we manage. This is something distinctive in the investment management field.

Richard Wilson: Over the past three years there have been many discussions about hedge funds readjusting their management and performance fee calculations to take a more long-term interest alongside the investor. The argument is that if a hedge fund manager could potentially take on a large amount of risk with other people's money, they may do so to aim for a $100 million-plus payday. What has your firm put into place to align the financial incentives of your fund more closely with your investors?

David R. Koenig: Our annual management fees range from 0.5 percent to 2.0 percent of beginning period assets under management (AUM). Management fees are maximized when we do well. If we don't perform, we give some of our fees back to the customer via a reduced management fee. "Doing well" means hitting both our return and risk targets.

Similarly, incentive fees are earned only after we pass a hurdle rate. When they are earned, rather than being paid in cash, they are paid in fund interests with a hard lock for two years from the date of payment. This further aligns the manager's interests with those of our investors. In addition, incentive fees are capped to prevent any conflicting incentive toward excessive risk taking. An example is the following table, which comes from two of the funds we have been engaged to manage.

	Hurdle Rate of Return	Share of Excess	Rate of Return Cap for Incentive Fee Calculations	Effective Cap on Incentive Fees
Relative Return Strategy	2.0% above the index	50%	8.0% above the index	3% of beginning of period AUM
Absolute Return Strategy	5.0%	30%	15%	3% of beginning of period AUM

Richard Wilson: Others have also stressed the importance of using trusted service providers who have expertise and a history of client relationships in the hedge fund space. Do you agree with this approach?

David R. Koenig: Separation of duties and the engagement of leading service providers are essential elements to an operationally sound and successful control environment. We agree wholeheartedly.

Richard Wilson: Would you agree with me that hedge funds need to be considering strong governance as a must-have instead of a nice-to-have in today's marketplace?

David R. Koenig: Effective corporate governance, while complex, is essential to the long-range success of any organization. Again, if you recognize that you are running a business, whose key asset is its clients, then the answer becomes clear.

CHAPTER SUMMARY

In this chapter we discuss some governance best practices that hedge funds can follow to improve their decision making, capital-raising abilities, and, most importantly, risk management environment. Some key lessons from this chapter include the following:

- Many small to medium-size hedge funds have poor internal financial controls, and few have independent boards that take the perspective of the investor in all decisions.
- The main purpose of an independent board for a hedge fund is to collectively be responsible for the central control of the fund by overseeing the affairs of the appropriate interests of the shareholders and relevant stakeholders while at all times ensuring protection of the investors.
- The board's primary duties are statutory obligations, strategic and financial matters, personnel matters, report monitoring and control responsibilities, annual review of composition and effectiveness of the board, and corporate governance.
- Employing hedge fund governance best practices not only protects your business from some types of operational and fraud risks, but it also helps position your firm when marketing, and it improves decision-making processes.

REVIEW QUESTIONS

1. No internal control structure can _____.
   a. Completely prevent fraud.
   b. Assure investors positive financial returns.
   c. Protect the capital within a hedge fund.
2. True or false: One of the reasons why fund governance is becoming more important is that funds of hedge funds were somewhat seen as the eyes and ears of smaller investors, but they have recently failed to conduct adequate due diligence and research.
3. Andrew Main suggests that a board should complete a strategic review once a _____.
   a. Month.
   b. Quarter.
   c. Year.
4. True or false: Independent boards of advisers should be constructed of one type of professionals: forensic accounting and audit professionals.

This type of professional will always serve both the fund and investors best.

5. It is suggested in this chapter that board meetings be conducted at least once per _____.
    a. Week.
    b. Month.
    c. Quarter.
    d. Year.

6. What does it mean to have a nonexecutive board of advisers?
    a. To have a board made up of professionals in other industries who bring a unique view of the business.
    b. To have a board made up of junior-level professionals with unique perspectives on improving business operations.
    c. To have a board which is made up of professionals who do not also serve as portfolio managers or executives within the day-to-day running of the fund.

7. The cost of building a good board should probably be around _____ per director on the board.
    a. $8,500
    b. $15,000
    c. $22,500
    d. $25,000

8. Good governance _____; poor governance _____.
    a. Costs lots of money, doesn't cost much.
    b. Is rare, is very common.
    c. Adds value, detracts from it.

9. True or false: David R. Koenig believes that while good governance is nice to have, it is not essential to the long-term success of a hedge fund.

10. Poorly governed funds are more likely to have _____ surprise _____.
    a. Large, losses.
    b. Small, losses.
    c. Large, gains.
    d. Small, gains.

Answers: To view the answers to these questions, please see http://HedgeFundTraining.com/Answers

CHAPTER **9**

Frequently Asked Hedge Fund Questions

You are your greatest asset. Put your time, effort, and money into training, grooming, and encouraging your greatest asset.
—Tom Hopkins

T his chapter covers the most frequently asked questions about hedge funds. Our company receives over 150,000 e-mails each year, many of them asking the same questions that are covered here in this chapter.

HEDGE FUNDS 101

Question: What is a hedge fund?

Answer: A hedge fund is a private investment vehicle in which investors in the fund typically are charged a management fee plus a performance-based fee. While this definition has been true for some time now, there are dozens of variations of hedge funds, and many look a lot like private equity funds and venture capital funds. While the hedge fund industry has been organically growing in real size, it is also growing simply due to the application of the name *hedge fund* to an increasing number of investment vehicles. Typical hedge fund management fees are between 1 and 2 percent, and typical performance fees range from 15 to 30 percent. Investors are drawn to hedge funds because they have strong incentives to perform very well in order to take down a large dollar figure as part of the performance fee charged by the fund. While some would say this is a light version of the definition, the truth is that the model has expanded in so many directions that any more details would leave out billions of dollars worth of hedge fund strategies and models. The industry truly is defined by the fees the funds now charge and how those are structured to the investor.

Question: What is a fund of hedge funds?

Answer: A fund of hedge funds is an investment fund that allows a single investor broad access to many different hedge funds through one investment. The fund of hedge funds typically researches dozens or hundreds of hedge fund managers in order to optimize and invest for clients in a basket of well-performing hedge funds. A fund of hedge funds earns fees on top of the hedge fund management and performance fees already embedded in this type of investment. Investors are drawn to funds of hedge funds for the superior research and due diligence conducted and the diversity of hedge fund risk exposures that may be found in these vehicles.

Question: What is the difference between a multistrategy hedge fund and a fund of hedge funds?

Answer: A multistrategy hedge fund is a fund that runs multiple strategies such as long/short, 130/30, global macro, merger arbitrage, and so on, all in the same fund. This fund will typically charge a single layer of fees similar to any other hedge fund. This contrasts with a fund of hedge funds, which could be focused on one or two hedge fund strategies or many in a diversified model where an additional layer of fees is applied for the research, due diligence, and risk management research that went into constructing the portfolio of unique hedge fund managers in the fund.

Question: What hedge fund books would you recommend reading?

Answer: We offer a free-to-download 200-plus-page e-book on hedge funds, online at http://HedgeFundsBook.com. We also suggest visiting HedgeFundBookStore.com to review the short list of books that our team has selected for the CHP Designation Program. We reviewed over 55 books on hedge funds before selecting this group of texts for our training program.

Question: What is the role of an institutional investment consultant?

Answer: Institutional investment consultants are investment advisers to mainly large institutional investors such as pension funds, foundations, endowments, or family offices. Investment decisions are often made with the advice of these consultants, and sometimes parts or whole portfolios are placed under the control and investment decision making of these institutional consultants. Hedge fund managers are typically interested in developing strong relationships with institutional consultants because those managers with over $80 million or $100 million in assets can often build relationships with these consultants and possibly gain allocations from their institutional investor clients.

Question: How strong is the industry outside of the United States and Europe?

Answer: The hedge fund industry is diverse and spread out around the world. Australia, Brazil, South Africa, and Russia are all hubs of CTA fund and hedge fund activity. I met with a CTA fund in São Paulo, Brazil, last year for lunch and he mentioned that he personally knew of over 300 funds similar to his which are based in São Paulo. While many international locations may lack more than a handful of $750 million-plus hedge funds, they house thousands of small to medium-size hedge fund managers who together control a lot of assets and hire a respectable number of employees as well.

Question: What is the quickest way to gain more knowledge about hedge funds right now?

Answer: Many times I hear from professionals who have been reading HedgeFundBlogger.com, who have read this book, or who read our hedge fund e-book and they are hungry to learn more. Here are my four top tips on moving up the learning curve on everything hedge funds:

1. Our free 200-page hedge fund e-book (http://HedgeFundsBook.com).
2. Sign up for Google Alerts for the terms "Hedge Fund," "Hedge Funds," and so on. This will allow Google to e-mail you once a week as new Web stories or blog articles come out on hedge funds.
3. Subscribe to HedgeFundBlogger.com and receive our daily e-mail newsletter about the hedge fund industry.
4. Subscribe to five educational blogs on the topic of hedge funds. Suggestions include HedgeFundBlogger.com, Fintag.com, FT AlphaVille (FTalphaville.ft.com), and the Albourne Village newsletter found at Village.Albourne.com.

HEDGE FUND OPERATIONS

Question: I am a solid trader with a solid back-tested model. Should I start a hedge fund?

Answer: The hard truth is probably not. Most traders do not have the level of pedigree or supporting capital that is needed to launch and grow a fund from the ground up. That said, new hedge funds are launched daily, and many funds do make it to a profitable level of assets under management (AUM) and do very well. It is important to do your research before you spend any money on service providers or legal formation. Work up your budget, write a business plan, write a marketing plan, meet with potential friends and family investors, and speak with other small hedge fund managers. Raising capital and growing a long track record that will attract investors both take a long time and a lot of patience.

Question: What is one operational fund management process you could provide me with that I can take away and really use in my business today? I need something low cost as we manage less than $100 million in assets as a fund.

Answer: One person who has affected me in business has been William Edward Deming. He once said, "If you can't describe what you are doing as a process, you don't know what you are doing." I think this also goes along with another popular business quote: "What gets documented gets improved."

Most investment funds and family offices that I have worked with do not have an investor cultivation process or pipeline drawn out as a process. They do not have their ongoing investor communication strategy documented, and in many places the only documentation of their investment process is at a very high level in their marketing materials. I think many hedge funds, portfolio managers, and capital raisers could benefit from using PowerPoint presentations or a free program such as Bubbl (www.bubbl.us) to document their processes.

This documenting of critical processes takes little time and costs nothing to do, but it allows you to step back from the process and evaluate it, improve it, or delegate where appropriate. Our firm recently used Bubbl and PowerPoint together to describe a business process we were completing ourselves, and we were able to use this not only internally but also externally as we trained a third party to whom we decided to outsource some of this work.

The processes I have found valuable to document are:

- Investor acquisition process.
- Current investor communication strategy.
- Hiring new employees.
- Managing your portfolio on an ongoing basis.

Question: What exactly does a fund administration firm do? What is the scope of their services?

Answer: A fund administration firm helps with the day-to-day operations of running a hedge fund. Activities that typical administration firms may take on for a fund include:

- Monthly accounting.
- Tax preparation assistance.
- Processing of subscriptions and redemptions.
- Third-party controls.
- Audit assistance.
- Anti–money laundering (AML) compliance.

- Investor communications.
- Daily reconciliation of trades.
- Employee Retirement Income Security Act (ERISA) tracking.
- Operational assistance.
- Management company accounting.

Question: What are your top five pieces of advice for a hedge fund that is just now starting up?

Answer: Our firm speaks with over 300 hedge fund start-ups and emerging hedge fund managers each year. We typically hear from managers when they need help selecting service providers such as a formation attorney or prime brokerage firm, or we get requests to help these funds raise capital for their new funds. Here are our top five tips for hedge fund start-ups:

1. It is harder to raise capital than you think, so get all of your capital-raising processes, investor database resources, and sales professionals in place before you start your fund.
2. Focus on developing a unique investment process and competitive advantage in the industry: What unique edge can you constantly be building?
3. Risk management and institutionalization are key for your fund. Focus on how to be more transparent than your competitors. Decide where you can invest early in technology, research, or pedigree to raise the institutional quality of your fund offering.
4. Investors want to see that you have skin in the game. Make sure you do have some of yourself invested and communicate that to investors.
5. Face-to-face relationships work. Meet with as many potential investors, service providers, and consultants in person as possible. This leads to more trust, momentum, and productivity in everything you touch.

Question: Do you have any suggestions on how we could run our hedge fund business better from an operational or business point of view so that we are seen as more of an authority in the industry?

Answer: Sure. One way in which people are influenced every day is through our orienting reflex. The orienting reflex is the process we go through while reacting to something novel, new, or mysterious. It is what makes first dates, roller coasters, and vacations to exotic islands so enjoyable.

When a loud alarm goes off we stop and ask ourselves why it is going off and whether it has any impact on us. If you are in the middle of a movie at your local theater and the fire alarm starts to go off, everyone will look around for a minute before taking action. Each person is orienting themselves to this new situation and combination of variables, and they are looking for instructions from other people's actions, their past experiences, or some sort of authority such as a movie theater employee. This very moment, while the movie audience is determining what to do next, is when they are most easily influenced. This same rule applies to changes in stock market conditions and the reaction of Wall Street analysts and investment news broadcasters.

If you can be the person to suggest a strategy or provide additional credible evidence when others are still orienting to a new environment, you can be very influential very quickly.

You can apply this in your fund by being the first to address an industry development such as new investor regulations, or an industry-changing fraud event like Madoff. Interpret these events and focus on making sense of what will likely come next. This can be done on a smaller level with events that come up each quarter in the industry.

Question: How can I network with other hedge fund managers and industry professionals?

Answer: The best way to network with other hedge fund managers and industry professionals is through the Hedge Fund Group, a free-to-join association of industry professionals. This group now has over 30,000 members from around the world, and you may join today by visiting HedgeFundGroup.org and clicking on the "Join" link at the top right-hand side of the home page.

HEDGE FUND MARKETING AND SALES

 BONUS VIDEO MODULE

To watch a 45-minute video on hedge fund marketing best practices, please type this URL into your Web browser: http://HedgeFundTraining.com/Capital-Raising-Strategies

Question: What does a typical third-party marketing arrangement look like? What are the payouts like?

Answer: Third-party marketing arrangements typically involve the marketer receiving 20 percent of both the management and performance fees on assets raised for five years, seven years, or in perpetuity for as long as the investor remains invested in the fund. In addition to the fee sharing, most third-party marketers will also charge some level of a retainer, which can range from \$1,000/month to \$12,000/month, to help cover the ongoing marketing costs of the marketer. If your hedge fund is looking to engage a third-party marketer, please read some of our free advice on this niche area of business at ThirdPartyMarketing.com, a free educational e-magazine on the third-party marketing industry.

Question: We are looking for capital. Would a hedge fund invest in my real estate venture or private company?

Answer: The hedge fund universe is diverse and there are hedge funds that invest in real estate or in private companies, but these are few and far between. You will need to obtain a specialized database of these types of hedge fund managers, or screen carefully in one of the large hedge fund database providers found online. For further information on databases, both free and paid, please see InvestorDatabases.com, HedgeFund.Net, Hedge-FundResearch.com, or FamilyOfficesDatabase.com for more information.

Question: How long will it take us to raise capital after we launch our fund?

Answer: The sales cycle is six to nine months long in retail channels and 9 to 18 months long in institutional channels. This assumes that your fund has a three- to five-year or longer track record and a high enough level of AUM to approach each of these markets. Raising capital from investors other than friends and family in your first two years is very challenging. The best route of action is to consider seed capital or approach high net worth (HNW) accredited investors for potential investments. Even the most experienced third-party marketers and capital raisers need 9 to 12 months to close on a significant level of assets, and many need two to three years to really work through their contact Rolodex and use all of their methods of attracting capital to clients. It is important to know this up front when you start a fund, both for budgeting and for setting reasonable expectations of anyone you hire or bring on as a third-party marketer for the fund.

Question: Can you provide us some tips on how to develop relationships with investors? Is there a process we could follow at a very high level?

Answer: Yes, there is. I was making my way through some marketing training materials last year from Mr. Frank Kern and came across a marketing process which may seem somewhat like common sense, but it helps to think about these things to ensure that you are presenting a complete marketing message to your potential fund investors. In the marketing training program, Kern suggests you follow this four-step process while moving your prospects through different phases of engaging your firm:

1. *Interest and desire.* Provide a white paper, speech, update on your perspective of the markets, which catches the attention of your potential investor.

2. *Trust*. Develop a relationship with the potential investor. Build trust by providing client quotes, industry recommendations, and comparison analytics between your fund and others.
3. *Proof*. Show proof that your fund has a high pedigree team, detailed consistent investment processes in place, and an advantage of some type which can be tangibly displayed or confirmed.
4. *Sample*. Allow the investor to start with a small minimum investment, provide examples of what other investors like them have done in the past, or present case studies on three different types of typical investors that you serve so they can imagine being in that position.

The descriptions of these four steps are less important than the process itself. If you can grab the attention of the investor, build a relationship with them, provide proof of your abilities and performance, and then combine that with a sample, you will be several steps ahead of much of your competition.

 BONUS VIDEO MODULE

To watch a video on the strategy of similar others, please type this URL into your Web browser: http://HedgeFundTraining.com/Marketer

Question: How could we improve our PowerPoint pitch book for investors?

Answer: This will depend on its current state, your strategy, and your target investors, but following are a few of the most common tips that I often provide to fund managers looking to improve their PowerPoint presentations:

- *Quarterly update*. Most potential investors will have already seen your one-pager, which is updated monthly. The presentation should mention your performance but the main purpose of it is to present your team's pedigree, investment process, and risk controls. Hire a professional editor to spend an hour reviewing the presentation after each major review; this costs less than $100.
- *Three areas of focus*. As previously indicated, the three areas of focus in the PowerPoint presentation should be team pedigree and experience, investment process, and risk controls. Many managers tend to be very

high level while describing their investment process and risk controls, frequently using terms that are seen too often in generic industry presentations. You have to let out enough of your secret sauce in your marketing materials so that others know there is actually something there. Solid returns alone, even in these recent markets, are not enough. You must provide some explanation of your consistent process, system, and parameters for operating. Here is some advice on each of the three most important sections of your PowerPoint presentation:

1. *Team pedigree.* Take the time to describe all of the relevant experience that your team holds, and try to explain those experiences in ways that mesh well with your firm's investment process and approach to managing risk. Many types of experience can be valuable to managing a portfolio of investments, but sometimes that connection needs to be spelled out in the presentation. If after creating this section you realize that your team consists of just one or two professionals without a long industry track record, consider beefing up your close advisory board with industry veterans and experts in risk and portfolio management. Many times investors will ask how much of a fund principal's own assets are invested in the funds. Regardless of the exact dollar amount, if 80 to 90 percent or more of your own liquid assets are invested in this fund, check with your compliance officer about noting this in your presentation materials. Many investors turn to hedge funds due to an alignment of interests, and providing evidence of this in your fund sometimes helps. It is important to retain capital-raising talent as well, but without proper portfolio and risk management professionals or advisory professionals in place, you may just spin your wheels. As you expand your team, be sure to include a team hierarchy tree in your presentation. This may include your advisory team and a few service providers or research groups with whom you work daily and upon whom you rely for operations.

2. *Investment process.* This is most commonly the area of PowerPoint presentations that needs improvement. I have found it easiest to try to break your investment process into three to five steps, which could then be broken down further during a due diligence phone call or in meetings with potential investors. I would start with a single page displaying the three- to five-step investment process your firm uses, followed by one to two pages explaining each step of the process in great detail. Describe the tools you use, the decision-making process, research inputs, parameters for refining the universe of potential investments, and triggers that may affect how the portfolio is constructed at each step. Following this, consider adding another page

to the PowerPoint on buy and sell decision triggers: When do you trim a position? When do you sell? When are positions cleared out completely? What stop-loss provisions are in place? Providing a few trading case studies in this part of the PowerPoint may be helpful. Use real-life examples from the previous quarter and update these frequently so that analysts will be able to read into your decisions in context of the recent market conditions.

3. *Risk management techniques.* Risk management techniques can be placed in a separate section of the presentation or tacked onto the end of your investment process section in the PowerPoint. It is hard to go overboard on explaining with granularity what risk management techniques your firm employs. Start with the status quo: What tools, research, stop-loss provisions, and systems are used? Next move on to proprietary models you may be using, exclusive trading research, or experience that provides additional insight into how you manage risk in your portfolio.

- *More is more.* It is often better to go overboard with details on your investment processes and risk management details than not to provide enough information. That said, never let the presentation grow to over 25 pages unless you have three or more products being presented in a single presentation. Getting your PowerPoint right is about balancing transparency and granularity against confusion and information overload. Everyone is busy, and often getting someone to invest three minutes to review your one-pager can be a challenge of its own.

Creating a solid PowerPoint presentation is a task of continual improvement, but if you start with these tips it should set you above 50 percent of the sub–$200 million hedge funds that we often speak with.

Question: What should we look at while interviewing a third-party marketer we may hire?

Answer: Evaluating a potential marketer should be as rigorous as completing a request for proposal (RFP) for an institutional consultant. A partnership is being formed, and investing time and money with the wrong professionals can be expensive in terms of both real dollars and opportunity costs. Areas to cover while conducting due diligence on a third-party marketer include:

- Past work experience.
- Current licensing and broker check.
- Asset-raising history throughout their careers.
- Asset-raising track record while working together in the firm.

- Referrals from past hedge fund clients.
- Number of years experience.
- Scope of their distribution channel expertise.
- Number of total current clients.
- Potential commitment of time in terms of hours per week and duration of the contract.
- Personality and culture of the third-party marketing group.

Question: What trends have you seen in terms of the types of investors now out there in the hedge fund industry?

Answer: What I find is that overall, while most marketers' experiences are very similar, each investor is different, just as the due diligence processes in different firms vary. Hedge fund investors typically fall into one of these four categories:

1. *The "Follow me" hedge fund investor.* Most of these investors make up your pool of family, friends, co-workers, and people you interact with regularly. Usually, these people don't understand how to perform the necessary due diligence in making a decision to invest. This group also tends to make assumptions. For example, if a manager holds a degree from Harvard or has experience from a top financial firm, this fact alone would persuade these investors to follow suit, ignoring the probability of fraud. In addition, they heavily rely on personal acquaintance and recommendations from either you or someone you may know. If you ask for a check, and they trust you, this group will most likely give one to you.
2. *The "Send me a prospectus" hedge fund investor.* This group is a bit more sophisticated and conducts a minimum amount of due diligence into the manager's performance. Once they are satisfied with the performance on paper, they will meet with and usually shower the manager with questions regarding every aspect of the fund, including returns, performance, strategies, and risks. What is written and spoken by the manager is taken on faith and the information is not properly verified by the investor.
3. *The investigating hedge fund investor.* This type of investor is sometimes considered a nuisance by busy professionals who might be caught off-guard by his questions. Not only will the investor keep the manager's number on speed dial, but he will perform due diligence above and beyond the previous types and will go so far as to understand the entire operation of the fund as if he were the manager. This type will also interview members of the manager's staff and will look into the balance

sheet, cash controls, reporting, and other functions not directly related to performance.

4. *The independent hedge fund investor.* The due diligence collected by this investor is thoroughly reviewed independently. Investors in this category know that independent opinions are extremely important. They will contact the auditor, custodian, and administrator in addition to the SEC and/or state securities agency. They won't sign on the dotted line until they are satisfied that they have independently verified everything that matters, including assets under management, returns, and even a year-end audit. They fully understand the risks that are involved.

Nobody likes to be put in a box, but it is important to realize that the types of investors can vary widely, so you should prepare an array of marketing materials, from brief one-pagers to very detailed institutional-quality PowerPoint presentations and third-party analyses for those most scrutinizing parties. My experience has been that marketing materials that are first built to the highest standard and later summarized into smaller, dumbed-down pieces can be very effective and versatile.

Question: When marketing to financial advisers for your hedge fund, what steps do you need to take dealing with these guys? Is it any different from dealing with family offices?

Answer: Marketing to financial advisers is much different from marketing to single and multifamily offices. Here are the main differences between the two:

- Family offices have more established due diligence procedures, often involving consultants or internal analysts who do nothing but look at hedge funds or alternative investment products.
- Financial advisers have lower minimum asset levels for what they will consider investing. Ninety percent of family offices only seriously consider investing in hedge funds with at least $75 to $100 million, and many require $250 $300 million or even $1 billion in assets under management.
- Family offices are more tight-lipped. It will take more effort to develop a relationship, meet in person, and get clear feedback on why a hedge fund is or is not a good fit for what they are looking for.
- Family offices are harder to identify in the first place. Financial advisers are easier to find, there are more of them, and they advertise more openly. Some family offices advertise but many stay below the radar, and some purposely don't even have a web site.

- While family offices service high net worth investors almost exclusively, many financial advisers work with a broad spectrum of client types. This might require more caution by them and by your fund in marketing products to them. It might also mean sorting through more financial advisers to find one with several HNW clients.
- In my experience, financial advisers seem much more sensitive to and motivated by how they will earn a commission or income from the transaction, whereas many family offices charge rich enough fees that this is less of an issue.
- While some financial advisers may take 16 to 24 months to really get on board with a relevant hedge fund manager, understand your investment process, and possibly invest, most will come to terms a bit before then. Family offices, by contrast, often take 18 to 24 months just to complete their due diligence and committee meetings; it is a very long sales process.
- Both family offices and financial advisers require genuine relationship-building efforts and tenacity.

From a legal standpoint there may be other precautions your fund should take, but I am not a legal expert so I can't provide any guidance in that space.

Question: Richard, from a capital-raising perspective, what would you say is the time frame to raise money (say $10 million or more) for a small, start-up hedge fund with no name recognition and with principals who have no name recognition and no pedigree in the alternative investment world? I would say 12 months at best. What do you think?

Answer: I would say 16 to 20 months would be realistic if they keep their heads down and have a great team and a solid investment process. Those are big if's, though—it is easy to get distracted or discouraged. The first fund I marketed took nine months straight of cold-calling, e-mails, and conferences to raise a single dollar, but after 18 months we were raising $1 million a week in new assets.

Question: Do you have a quick takeaway lesson that I could apply to my business development work for our family of hedge funds? There is always so much to get done and so little time to do it. What advice would you give us?

Answer: Following is a quote I used recently while speaking with an investment fund manager who was looking to raise capital. He was doing so by approaching every investor he could possibly speak to. He was explaining how his firm has so few resources compared to their $1 billion competitors.

You can take a $5 disposable camera and take it out of the box, stand 10 feet from a building, and take a great picture that will be developed and look good if not great. You could stand in that same position with a $10,000 camera with every gadget, lens, and a tripod, and it will not take as good a picture if you do not do one thing: Focus.

—Brian Tracy

The point: You can beat your competition with a smaller staff, less financial resource, and less experience if you just learn to focus. Focus on your top prospective investors, focus on local potential investors, and focus exclusively on the types of investors that are most likely to make allocations to your fund. If you can dial in on these three areas—your hot prospect list, local investors, and the right investor mix (family offices, wealth management, pension funds, etc.)—then you can really cover a lot of ground quickly.

Question: For this question and answer exchange I actually went to an outside expert, Richard Dukas from Dukas PR, who works with many medium- and large-size hedge fund managers, and I asked him: Why should hedge funds invest in PR, especially when their ability to speak with the press is restricted by law in many places?

Answer: Presently, most new hedge funds are launched with money from friends and family, while more established players can launch new funds from a pool of existing investors. Hedge funds are prohibited from advertising and marketing. (Once contacted by a potential investor, a hedge fund can send out marketing material.) Thus, in order to attract new investors, hedge funds need to find a way to get their name out there. One way, of course, is through the media.

Most financial journalists have contact with a hedge fund manager or two. These managers are excellent sources of information, though much of it is negatively directed toward companies. As such, much of the back-and-forth between the media and hedge fund managers is off the record. The SEC's new rules, however, are aimed at transparency. With competition among hedge funds fierce, it certainly behooves hedge fund managers to use their investment expertise to help the public, and drum up investors in the process.

Most hedge fund managers are still extremely reticent when it comes to speaking to the media. What I've found is that it's very difficult to solicit managers to work with a PR firm.

Dukas says that the reticence comes from a feeling that hedge fund managers should be secretive and not share their ideas with anyone but their own investors. However, the new SEC regulations, combined with the movement toward activist investing, may change that. Maybe [hedge fund managers will realize] what they're doing is not so secretive after all.

As an example of a hedge fund that has embraced the concept of working with the media, look no further than our client Haven Advisors, which has racked up considerable press over the past few years.

I mentioned that competition among hedge fund managers is fierce, and it's not going to get easier. For example, Janus Capital, one of the world's largest mutual fund managers, recently launched a long/short mutual fund with the goal of absolute return. In other words, Janus is offering investors access to a mutual fund that acts in the same way that most hedge funds act, but without the stiff management fees. More mutual funds such as the one launched by Janus should hit the market this year, opening up a whole new pool of investors to the idea of hedge funds. The biggest reason, however, I feel that hedge fund managers need PR people is the rise of activist investing.

Activist investing is not new, but for whatever reason, hedge funds ratcheted up what we call "cage rattling" last year. The normal sequence goes something like this:

1. A hedge fund builds up a large stake in a company by buying stock on the open market because the fund feels the stock is undervalued.
2. The fund approaches management and the board of the company and offers suggestions about how to unlock the value of the stock.
3. Management and the board ignore the fund, though in a noncombative way.
4. The hedge fund gets tired of being jerked away, and publicizes its cage rattling through an SEC filing (usually attaching letters that it has sent the company's management and board).

In some cases, companies capitulate, mostly because other investors have latched onto the ideas put forth by hedge funds and begun demanding change. In other cases, companies will battle hedge funds, hoping to eventually shake them out as investors. Regardless of the eventual outcome, hedge funds need public relations people because companies inherently have a public relations machine built into their organization. While hedge fund managers complain in SEC filings and on conference calls, companies are utilizing their public relations resources to work the media and investors. One good example of the company-versus-fund public relations mentality is Time Warner.

Last year, billionaire corporate raider Carl Icahn built a more than 3 percent stake in Time Warner. In doing so, Icahn began demanding a number of changes, including a massive stock buyback and a better monetization of Time Warner's AOL asset. Time Warner gave in partly, announcing a $12.5 billion stock repurchase. (Stock repurchases help companies boost earnings by giving existing shareholders more equity for their shares, that is, existing shares become more valuable because there are fewer shares outstanding when the company buys back stock.) Time Warner, however, didn't do everything that Icahn asked.

When Time Warner announced a wide-ranging pact with Google, Icahn was seemingly furious, warning the company ahead of the deal that it was making a mistake. Time Warner, with its PR machine in full gear, basically blew off Icahn, who was working the media in his own way. The end result was a deal that Time Warner wanted and was generally hailed for, and a deal that Icahn apparently hates. At last check, Icahn was having difficulty finding potential candidates for a reconstituted board that he wants to install at Time Warner. Negative PR toward Icahn, no doubt, has contributed to this difficulty.

The main point to take home here is that there are public relations strategies and campaigns which hedge fund managers can keep in mind and follow. There are ethical and legal ways to promote or position a fund; it just takes someone who has been there before to accomplish this.

Question: How are in-house hedge fund marketers typically compensated?

Answer: There are half a dozen models for compensating in-house marketers, but typically it is structured around a relatively low base salary combined with a small percentage of fees from new assets raised and trails from assets raised over the past two to five years. For example, a junior to mid-level marketer may be paid a $52,000 base salary, receive 5 percent of fees on new assets raised this year, and receive 3 percent of fees from assets raised over the past five years. All of this may change drastically based on the size of the hedge fund, the investor distribution channel targeted, the track record of the fund, and the typical sales cycle and allocation sizes that the fund has recently experienced over the past two years. Some marketers, if deeply experienced, ask for an equity partnership in the hedge fund to be vested after two to four years, assuming they raise enough capital to push them past a certain threshold set in the employment contract. This is most likely the case with small- to medium-size hedge funds, which cannot afford to otherwise pay for this type of help.

Question: I have done a lot of cold-calling for the hedge fund I am marketing. Do you have any cold-calling-related advice or tips, either for us as a team or for me individually?

Answer: Yes, I do have some tips, seven of which come immediately to mind:

1. Don't ask the prospect, "How are you doing?" You don't care how they are doing. If you cared you would have done some research on the

company first and you would have something more intelligent to ask them. This might sound harsh but it is true. Do your homework first.

2. Keep in mind that thousands of people cold-call and several people are probably calling the same or very similar prospects as the ones you are approaching. Everyone plays the numbers game, and it is natural to have your calls or e-mails go unanswered. The goal is to develop enough perceived value so they will take your call the next time or call you when they are ready to buy your product or service.

3. Shoot for 30 to 80 phone calls a day. More is not always better, but trying to do 6 to 10 calls an hour will keep you on your toes and always dialing more prospects. Create a game out of the process.

4. Smile while you dial. The tone of your voice and word choice both change based on your own feelings and facial expressions. Be happy and love your job, and the people on the other end of the phone will take notice.

5. Call the CEO. Always call the CEO. They are the masters of every other department and if a call or e-mail gets forwarded from them down to a vice president or department manager, it is much more likely to get responded to than coming in through an analyst or associate with the firm.

6. Set the table. This is a point Brian Tracy makes in the book, *Eat That Frog* (Berrett-Koehler, 2007). Sit down every night and take 20 minutes to plan out your work for the next day. Break the day into 30-minute sessions of complete focus, completing your most important tasks before most people even get to work in the morning.

7. Prepare a standard e-mail that you send out before you call. Anyone can send a great follow-up e-mail to a phone call—the trick is getting the prospect on the phone in the first place. Don't have them refuse to take your call because they do not know who you are. E-mail the prospect first, introducing yourself and stating, in three to five sentences or less, why you would like to have a five-minute conversation. Then call 10 minutes after sending the e-mail out.

What is interesting about making all of these phone calls is listening to how differently people sound and react during these conversations.

I remember one day last year I called someone who was unqualified. It turned out that their company didn't even provide the type of service I was hoping to discuss. I made a joke about sending him a personal check or Paypal payment to provide me with the type of contact I needed to connect with, and it worked. I was not trying to be manipulative by forcing myself to be funny to get information, I just made a dumb joke. Even after this was obvious, this individual asked me what I needed and ended up connecting me with a very valuable contact. He also asked where I lived, where I grew up, and if I had a wife or any kids. I was shocked, not while talking to him but after I hung up. In eight months of making over 600 phone calls, I had never once had someone be so friendly and up-front like that. It was a refreshing change from the monotone burnt-out tone of voice I usually end up listening to. What is important is not what happened during this phone call but after I realized how valuable a contact he had given me. I felt strongly obligated to thank him or repay him in some way.

This has taught me to always see the humor in situations and give value away freely to those in need of help.

One last unrelated sales phone call lesson I have learned is that if you have highly qualified the *end* person that you are trying to reach, they will be happy to talk to you because your service is relevant to them and necessary for their success.

Question: What advice can you give me about networking with investors and other hedge fund managers?

Answer: The best part about writing in HedgeFundBlogger.com each day is getting the 200 to 300 e-mails a day from hedge fund professionals, investors, and students in finance. One of the most frequent questions I get is "Can you help our hedge fund raise capital from new investors?" I usually refer these people on to others, as the firm I am with already has our hands full in raising capital right now for a set number of funds.

I recently read a quote, though, from Woody Allen: "Eighty percent of success in life is simply showing up." Show up at your local CHP and hedge fund association meetings. Meet face-to-face with local financial advisers, institutional consultants, and foundations. We are looking for something more out of our jobs than a simple paycheck, and if your fund offers potential investors something in the parameters of what they are allowed to choose, they might choose your product simply because of your relationship. My favorite sales author, Jeffrey Gitomer, always says that "all things being equal, people like to do business with their friends . . . and all things *not* being equal, people still like to do business with their friends." My quick advice to most funds is to make sure your compliance details are in order and then start showing up everywhere you can to start building long-term, multiyear relationships in the industry. Maybe even join the Hedge Fund Group for free and start networking there.

Question: Why is capital raising so difficult?

Answer: Here's one take:

- Forty-four percent of all salespeople quit trying after the first call.
- Twenty-four percent quit after the second call.

- Fourteen percent quit after the third call.
- Twelve percent quit trying to sell their prospect after the fourth call.

This means 94 percent of salespeople quit before the fifth phone call, while 60 percent of all sales are made after the fourth call. This means that the overwhelming majority of hedge fund sales professionals don't even give themselves a shot at selling their products.

Question: Do you have any advice for creating a contract to work with a third-party marketer? This is our first time going through this process.

Answer: If you are hiring a third-party marketer for the first time, move slowly. Meet with your legal counsel before you even begin to speak with third-party marketing firms so that you know what questions to ask up front. If possible have a contract you would prefer to work under on hand so you do not have to take their contract and modify it to your needs. Interview and meet face-to-face with several third-party marketers who have references and track records of raising assets so you can start to pick out the smooth talkers from those with real evidence of having successfully raised capital. Typically it is a bad idea to pay front-heavy partnership fees or service initiation fees, but it is relatively common to pay some sort of ongoing monthly or quarterly retainer to those firms that are spending time on marketing your fund every day. If you would like to learn more about third-party marketing before moving forward, please see ThirdPartyMarketing.com for hundreds of free related tips, articles, and resources.

Question: What is the difference between brokers, third-party marketers, and capital introduction professionals?

Answer: All three types of professionals raise capital for hedge funds. Brokers can sometimes be third-party marketers, but the term usually refers to more generic capital connectors or networkers in the industry who may be accustomed to being paid small lump sums instead of a small percentage of the management and performance fees over time. Third-party marketers are independent capital raisers who use their Rolodex and refined capital-raising processes to raise the AUM levels of several fund managers at any given time. Third-party marketers work with hedge funds, but they also may represent mutual funds, exchange-traded funds (ETFs), private equity groups, real estate investment trusts (REITs), and so on. Capital introduction teams are typically run inside of investment banks, trading houses, and prime brokerage shops. These *cap intro* teams, as they are often called, raise capital for their fund clients in an effort to keep them on their trading platform. The longer the fund remains trading in the platform, the more fees are generated for the trading firm that supports them.

HEDGE FUND CAREERS

 BONUS VIDEO MODULE

To watch a video on how to start a hedge fund career, please type this URL into your Web browser: http://HedgeFundTraining.com/Career

Question: How important is ethics or ethical policies in the hedge fund industry?

Answer: It's important. In the hedge fund industry you have one name and one reputation. If you ruin that, you could have influential people in the industry refusing to do business with you for 15 to 20 years after their initial opinion is formed. In such a competitive, close-to-the-vest industry where large profits can be made, the temptation to cut corners or look past fiduciary duties is sometimes too much.

The FBI recently had agents posing as a Florida-based hedge fund manager to nab 10 individuals in five kickback schemes connected to securities sales. The SEC charged 10 individuals and the U.S. Attorney's office charged six with criminal offenses.

In each case, the posing hedge fund manager told the targets that their actions must be kept secret because they violated his fiduciary duties, making it explicitly known that what was going on was illegal and unethical. "This case illustrates the Commission's ability to work together with criminal authorities in creative ways to uncover fraudulent schemes and to protect our markets," Linda Chatman Thomas, the head of the SEC's enforcement division, said.

Bottom line: If you are smart enough and hardworking enough to be successful, then you don't ever need to cut corners and blatantly break securities laws. Innovation and relationships are the competitive advantages that should make you extremely profitable, not cheating the system.

Question: Is there a professional training or certification program for hedge fund professionals?

Answer: Yes, for professional training programs of many types please visit HedgeFundTraining.com. This web site provides information on various hedge fund training programs available, including e-learning, DVD/workbook training, and seminar-based training for hedge fund industry professionals. For the hedge fund industry certification program, the Certified Hedge Fund Professional (CHP) Designation, please visit http://HedgeFundCertification.com.

 BONUS VIDEO MODULE

To watch a video on the credibility and global recognition of the CHP Designation, please type this URL into your Web browser: http://HedgeFundTraining.com/Credibility

Question: How do I get started working in the hedge fund industry?

Answer: There are many steps to starting a hedge fund career. Here are six of the first ones you should take:

1. The first thing you need to do to start a career in the industry is to read as much as you can about what is going on, how hedge funds operate, and where you may fit in. You will waste your own time and others' if you do not complete this first step. To learn as much as possible in a single month, read four to five books, subscribe to four or five free newsletters on hedge funds, and register for daily Google Alerts as well. Make sure to read at least two books on hedge fund careers and at least two books on hedge funds as an industry.
2. Finding an area in the industry that is a realistic entry point, includes potential work you are passionate about, and draws upon your past work experience and strengths. Gaining employment is a competitive process in this industry, and you will typically need to show evidence of commitment and loyalty to get in.
3. Identify two to three hedge fund industry career mentors. Identify a professor, hedge fund professional, or retired investment industry professional who could help provide you with advice and guidance on everything from crafting your resume to interviewing for open positions.
4. Complete one or more internships in the industry. It does not matter where you are located; there are hedge funds on every continent looking for help in completing their trading, potential investor, or competitive industry research. If you put yourself out there and do not give up, you will get into the industry and gain internships. At the beginning you may have to work for free to gain initial experience.
5. Develop a unique value proposition to potential employers. Reflect on your recently gained knowledge, natural abilities, past work experience,

and education. Decide how you could effectively present that as a great package to the hedge funds or service providers to whom you are applying for jobs. Do not be generic; come up with specific skills and abilities that allow you to stand out.

6. Some skills that stand out to hedge fund managers include quantitative modeling experience, Ivy League or advanced education, signs of loyalty or passion, retention of designations such as the CHP Designation, high-quality names from respected or local hedge funds on your resume, and a stomach for a high commission/profit-sharing type position.

 BONUS VIDEO MODULE

To watch a video on hedge fund internships, please type this URL into your Web browser: http://HedgeFundTraining.com/Internships

Question: What are the top mistakes often made by hedge fund career professionals?

Answer: There are five mistakes that our team sees hedge fund professionals and students making while trying to obtain employment in the industry. Our team receives over 50,000 career-related e-mails a year, and these mistakes are what we see most commonly made from this perspective of the industry:

1. *Annoying.* Every week we speak with professionals who are very passionate about working in the hedge fund industry. They will do almost anything to get a job working for a hedge fund, and they are eager to show this while networking and during interviews. The problem is that it can come off as overbearing and desperate. The more successful a hedge fund or any company is, the busier they typically will be, and the better the employer they will probably be as well. This means that the best employers have the least patience for those potential job candidates who send in three to four e-mails a week or leave two voice mails in a single day regarding open jobs or whether their resume has been reviewed.

2. *Overconfident.* One ironic aspect about growing a career or gaining knowledge on any niche subject is that the more you know, the more you realize you don't know very much. In other words, with each new skills or lesson that you pick up, you are opened to a dozen new skills

or lessons that you now realize you will have to master. Experienced business professionals and hedge fund managers know this, so coming off as all-knowing, or a master at anything, can often be taken as a sign of ignorance or a low tolerance for any teaching or instruction that may be required to complete the job well.

3. *Long resumes and e-mails.* This goes hand-in-hand with point 1 on not being annoying, but it so important that I am pulling it out as a separate point by itself. Many times when you think there are seven or eight important reasons why someone should interview or hire you, you may want to explain all of these in a single two- to three-page e-mail. This is a huge mistake; these e-mails are instantly deleted. Nobody in the industry has time to ready 20 essays by potential candidates on why they should be hired. Keep your e-mails down to three to five sentences at most, and be as concise and clear as possible.

4. *Generic.* Do whatever you can so that you are not generic. Nobody wants to hire someone who is just okay at many different things. You must stand out as being especially detail-oriented, teachable, passionate, or intelligent. Define your skill set and unique skills before the interview so you can ensure that the potential employer remembers them after the interview.

5. *Nothing but passion.* We see many professionals trying to enter the industry with nothing but a business degree and a lot of passion and desire. That is not enough, and you will fail if that is all you have. You must work your way into small internships and research projects. You must always be reading more about hedge funds and the specialized knowledge the job you are aiming for requires.

 BONUS VIDEO MODULE

To watch a video on top five hedge fund career mistakes, please type this URL into your Web browser: http://HedgeFundTraining.com/Mistakes

Question: Do you have a system for career development or improvement that you could share with us who are within our first five to seven years of our career?

Answer: Yes. There is a formula that I have used over the past seven years to help me build my resume, career, and now my own small business, and that is the SKAR formula. This is not a way to shortcut the hard work it takes to be successful, but rather a map of where you should invest your energy to increase the results you get in return.

SKAR Development Formula

Specialized Knowledge + Authority + Results

= Huge growth opportunities and faster development

within your career or business

SKAR Definitions

- *Specialized knowledge* means specific knowledge that is practical, functional, and very niche-specific to the area within which you work or the skill or ability you rely on to perform well. Specialized knowledge exists whether you are an airplane pilot, hedge fund analyst, or third-party marketer. The difference between having specialized knowledge and not having it could mean the difference between spending 18 months to complete a task or project and being able to develop strong client relationships and complete the same task in just three months. Having specialized knowledge lets you identify more opportunities, move more quickly on them, and execute with efficiency. When multiplied over several years, this puts you in a different league of competition. Some ideas on how you can further develop your specialized knowledge include:
  - Read two books/month for the next two years on the area of specialized knowledge that is going to benefit your business or career most.
  - Subscribe to three of the best newsletters from blogs or experts in your industry which are *not* rehashed press releases and garbage news. You learn close to nothing from reading the news. Instead, read insights, analyses, and white papers within these newsletters. There are at least two to three valuable free newsletters in each industry.
  - Complete a niche training and certification program specific to your area of specialized knowledge. Having a third party verify that you have obtained a certain level of specialized knowledge is *always* going to be more credible than your own statement that "I like to read books and e-mail newsletters, here is what I have read lately." Seek out an online certification program and start one within six months. This will force you to read and learn more within your niche.
  - Write one article a week on your thoughts, best practices, and lessons learned within your niche area of practice. Write anonymously by

creating a free blog at Blogger.com and start synthesizing what you
are learning and combining other ideas to create your own original
concepts (such as this blog post).

- *Authority* means creating structures around your firm or self so that
your knowledge and abilities are communicated in a way that positions you as an authority in your niche area. Ideally, this area lines
up one-to-one with your area of specialized knowledge, and it can be
the result of gathering this knowledge. Two professionals can hold the
same knowledge, yet while one write five books and completes over
50 press interviews a year, the other may be an armchair critic with
a small group of five to seven consulting clients. The better-positioned
professional will reap rewards from new opportunities coming toward
him, instead of the other way around.

  I was a competitive swimmer earlier in my life, and the best book
  I read on swimming was called *Total Immersion* by Terry Laughlin,
  and within the book he uses the phrase "swimming downhill." It was
  a way to swim so that your body is tilted forward and you literally cut
  continually downward into the water. If you get authority positioning
  right, it will be like you are swimming downhill. Jeffrey Gitomer is a
  great study of authority positioning. He started writing eight pages a
  day when he was 46 years old; now in his fifties he has more than 10
  best-selling books, and charges more than Colin Powell for speeches.
  The real important detail, though, is he *never* cold-calls anyone and
  never scrambles for new business. His phone literally rings off the hook
  with new opportunities, clients, and joint venture partnerships due to
  his positioning. He is swimming down a steep hill.

- Publish your own newsletter or blog. Even if you only publish something once every two weeks, having it and building it over time is
what is important.

- Interview one professional each month for your own blog or newsletter, explaining that you can't compensate them but as your web site
becomes more popular they may get some exposure, plus they can
have a copy of the recorded phone call transcript, MP3 file, or document that you type up. Interviewing experts is a shortcut to gaining
specialized knowledge and authority positioning quickly. Being able
to tell others that you have interviewed 20 of the top experts in the industry and that overall you found A and B and, most surprisingly, C,
is very powerful and carries authority. Note: The more strongly you
have fulfilled your work in building specialized knowledge, the more
willing these experts will be to connect with you and the more pointed
and refined your questions will be. Ever done an interview with a
journalist who has never worked in your field? Not always fun or

fulfilling to answer the basics, which can be looked up on Google in three seconds.

- Take what you have written within your own newsletter or blog and self-publish a book with 60 to 80 pages of single-spaced text. Anyone can do this for $15 at Lulu.com. Very simple—no more excuses that you do not have a book deal. I got my second big investment marketing contract partially because I had a self-published book in hand and someone gave me a chance based on my dedication to the niche. The book positions you as an authority.

- Create a one-page PDF list of all of your past clients. This can show depth, experience, and respect that others have given you by paying for your services and time in the past.

- Speak at conferences. It is relatively easy to land speaking spots at conferences, networking events, and seminars. Lots of professionals are looking for others with unique ideas and lessons to share. And again, teaching what specialized knowledge you have gained helps you connect and synthesize these ideas. If you are speaking to a crowd, you are in an authority position, and when you mention your speaking it adds credibility because others have stopped their business days and invested their valuable time to listen to what you have to say.

 BONUS VIDEO MODULE

To watch a video on authority construction tips, please type this URL into your Web browser: http://HedgeFundTraining.com/Authority

- *Results*. The importance of showing real, tangible results cannot be overstated. Finding ways to do this within service businesses, the fund management industry, or within certain areas of extreme confidentiality is challenging. Some types of tangible results that can be shared include:
  - An actual printed-out version of part of the service or end result of the product or service.
  - Video (preferred) or text (not as good) testimonials from past and current clients, the more specific to the immediate need or concern of your potential client or employer, the better—and the more numerous the testimonials, the better.
  - The first 15 to 20 percent of the product or your service given away for free on a trial basis. For example, offer a first month trial for $1, four weeks of free work or time so you can prove your worth to the client, and so on.

- Diverse and numerous case studies of past clients or employers. This proves that you work with firms with various needs and have found solutions for them, and it allows the reader of these case studies to imagine you solving their problem.
- A little tip, quick takeaway, or lesson within your sales letter or web site which provides the potential client with immediate benefit. This proves that you have the goods, are an authority, and do have their best interests in mind.

Another related topic that I don't have space to go into here is that underlying all three of these SKAR items is having the right habits. Habits have been shown to form 96 percent of what we do every single day. We tend to eat the same things, walk the same way, watch the same shows, and read the same types of books. As the quote goes, "First you form your habits, and then your habits form you." What business habits are you forming? What elements of the SKAR formula are you using each week? When you read this type of advice, are you thinking, "I already know this stuff," or "How good am I at that, and where could I improve?"

 BONUS VIDEO MODULE

To watch a video on the SKAR formula, please type this URL into your Web browser: http://HedgeFundTraining.com/SKAR

Question: Could you recommend three books on hedge fund careers?

Answer: Yes, to start with you could download a free e-book we offer on hedge funds online at http://HedgeFundsCareer.com. After that I would recommend reading *Hedge Me* by Claude Schwab (Lynx Media, 2006) and then *All About Hedge Funds* by Robert Jaeger (McGraw-Hill, 2002). These books combined will provide you with a good historic background of the industry, different perspectives on trends affecting hedge fund employment, and some tips on networking and connecting with hedge fund managers.

Question: I have been trying to get into the hedge fund industry for over four months now with no real progress. I'm about to give up and I just don't know whether there is any hope for someone like me with no Ivy League education or experience yet in the industry.

Answer: I made it into the industry and did well with neither of those resources under my belt. You probably can, too, if you want it badly enough. Here are some tips for building and keeping a positive attitude for when you are trying to overcome a challenge such as breaking into the hedge fund industry. This is what I do for my own goals and business:

- I work out at least three times a week.
- I have several three- to four-minute motivational podcasts or audio book clips on my iPod that I can listen to on the way to work.
- I read 15 pages of attitude-changing articles or books every morning while I am eating breakfast (see Jeffrey Gitomer's *Little Gold Book of YES! Attitude* [FT Press, 2006].).
- I have created a one-page laminated sheet with the top 50 business and sales lessons I have learned, and I have posted it in my shower, on my bathroom mirror, and behind my desk at work. I do my best to read this list twice a day to remind myself of what is important.
- I set BHAGS for myself—big, hairy, audacious goals, as described by Jim Collins in *Good to Great* (HarperBusiness, 2001). My current BHAGS? I want to become *the* expert in investment marketing and sales, run 50 investment web sites that rank in the top three slots of Google search results, and become a best-selling author.
- I try to find a lesson to be learned from each negative experience. If nothing else, a negative experience should always tell you something about yourself.
- I am always learning and exploring something new. First, it was getting into Harvard and moving to Boston; now it is learning all I can about investment marketing and sales, the psychology of influence, and Web marketing. As soon as you stop being curious and challenged you become stale and unmotivated.
- I cut off or drastically reduce communication with negative people.
- I don't watch the local news. It is worthless. How often do you see a news story about a generous church donation, a child winning a science project award, or an organ donor saving someone's life? Not nearly as often as a plane crash, fire, or robbery. If you have to get the local news, read it online for five minutes and save yourself some time.

Question: What would be your advice regarding third-party marketing? Is this trend dying out or growing? I am trying to learn more about the space.

Answer: If you are starting a third-party marketing career you are in good company: Dozens of highly experienced investment and hedge fund marketing/sales professionals are entering the industry each year. In terms of total firms offering services, the industry is growing by over 15 percent each year. While some professionals may leave an investment manager or hedge fund to start their own third-party marketing firm, many more first work or partner with an existing third-party marketing firm. The benefits of starting or working for a third-party marketing firm are many, and doing either is relatively easy to do. If you can raise capital and consistently bring in $100 million to $200 million/year, you can typically eliminate most types of political and corporate risks while having the potential of earning two to four times more than you would with the same experience while working for a large institution such as Morgan Stanley or Goldman Sachs. As the economy goes through this rough patch and bonuses are skimmed and 50-year old executives laid off, I see this trend of third-party marketing start-ups and career moves increasing. To learn more, please see http://thirdpartymarketing.com.

 BONUS VIDEO MODULE

To watch a video on hedge fund marketing careers, please type this URL into your Web browser: http://HedgeFundTraining.com/Careers

---

Question: I am a 38-year-old insurance executive and I have always wanted to work in the hedge fund industry. Do you believe it is too late to make a career change?

Answer: We get at least one question like this each month from professionals who work in investment banking, insurance, or corporate finance. The answer is no, it is not too late. It is an advantage if you have some corporate best practices training and some skill set that will help a fund manager grow their business. Oftentimes hedge fund managers need accountants, financial modelers, capital raisers, project managers, financial analysts, and detail-oriented investment professionals to help move their business forward. If you can't get an interview or position with a large hedge fund, make sure to try meeting with local service providers and small hedge funds start-ups or emerging hedge funds. A face-to-face meeting is worth 10 phone calls when it comes to networking.

Question: I am about to enroll in the CHP Designation Program. What does the program include? What is the process that I will go through?

Answer: The CHP Designation is an online self-study training and certification course on hedge funds. Once you join the program you will be sent a welcome letter thanking you for registering and providing you with bullet-point steps on how you can attend our networking events, gain access to our educational video content (over 100 videos and tools), receive our career coaching, acquire the required readings, access the mock exam, schedule your exam, and take advantage of CHP membership benefits. You then study using the video content, CHP study guide, and required readings, using our team as support when you have questions or get stuck on certain specific subjects. Your exam is conducted 100 percent online from wherever you are based. Over 40 percent of our participants complete the CHP Designation from outside of the United States. Learn more at http://HedgeFundCertification.com.

Question: What are your top tips for those who would like to start a career in the hedge fund industry? Anything else unique to what you have already mentioned?

Answer: Yes, here are some additional tips:

- Be absolutely sure you actually want to work in the hedge fund industry. As Yoda said, do or do not, there is no "try." If you try you will fail, because this industry is very competitive and it takes dedication and hard work to do well in the hedge fund industry.
- Become a student of the hedge fund industry. Study the industry every day by reading magazines, e-mail newsletters, books, and white papers. You need to speak the language of the industry.
- Use the three-circles strategy from Jim Collins. Collins suggests to move forward only with decisions that are a good fit with your background, involve something you are passionate about, and have the potential of being highly profitable. I use this strategy in my own life and you should, too, as you look at opportunities in this field.

Question: I am attending your Hedge Fund Premium seminar networking event next month in New York. I have never been to a networking event before and I wanted to see if you had a few quick tips on networking for me. Anything you can share?

Answer: If you're looking to enter the hedge fund industry either working directly for a firm or as a service provider to one, networking events and conferences are a great way to get your foot in the door.

Many professionals fail to take advantage of these opportunities, even those who attend. Here are five tips that should prepare you for attending a networking event or conference:

1. *Don't be shy.* Attending a hedge fund event is a good start, but you do not gain anything if you do not talk to other attendees, speakers, and sponsors. The event is only valuable if you make it valuable, so network and socialize with those around you.
2. *Don't scare people off.* Another mistake is to be too forward when approaching managers or service providers, especially if you are looking

to land a job in the hedge fund industry. Instead of sharing insights and thoughts on the industry, many young professionals will focus entirely on their own needs (a job) and ignore those managers or executives who are not currently hiring. This is the wrong mentality. Assuming you have been following the industry and paid good attention to the speaker, you will have a good starting point for initiating a conversation. Ask questions when appropriate and listen when the other person is speaking. If you are looking for a job, don't start a conversation by voicing that problem. Those who work in the industry are not paying to hear someone complain about not working in private equity. But you should mention it when the timing is appropriate.

3. *Get your name out there.* If you cannot find a hiring firm or no firms are interested in your product or service, don't despair—get your name out there. It may just be an inconvenient moment or the person you are talking with is not the right person at the firm. For example, if you are marketing your auditing service to a principal in charge of evaluating deals, he may not be interested. Give him your business card regardless; in another quarter the firm may be looking for a new auditor and still have your card. Even if you do not directly land a client through this method, it boosts your firm's or your own name recognition. If you're looking for a job (from analyst to executive), give your card out. Then when the firm is eventually hiring they will probably have your name on file.

4. *Prepare an elevator pitch.* It may not sound great, but you are a product that needs to be sold. Therefore you need to have a great elevator pitch that comes out effortlessly. Whether you are looking to network, marketing to investors, or job seeking, a solid elevator pitch is necessary. Be concise and include only essential information.

5. *Look and act like a professional.* Even though you are not at work when you're attending an event or conference, act like you are. You are meeting potential clients and partners, so you essentially are working. Wear a suit. If it's hot, as many crowded events are, at least make the initial effort and take off your coat once you sit down. Look your best (haircut, shave, and a suit) or no one will take you seriously. It's better to be overdressed than underdressed. Remember your manners, especially if it is a catered event, and use language that you would be comfortable using in the office.

Question: I am looking to work in the third-party marketing space. Do you have any career advice or book recommendations for those who want to work in third-party marketing? Do you have advice for getting a job in this niche industry?

Answer: There are no great books on third-party marketing that I am aware of. Everyone is pretty close-to-the-vest in the industry. I haven't found a great book on investment sales, either, but I know there are a few of those if you look around on Amazon. If you are looking for great books just on sales, I really like Jeffrey Gitomer's three books: *The Sales Bible* (HarperBusiness, 2008), *Little Red Book of Sales Answers* (FT Press, 2006), and *Little Gold Book of Yes! Attitude* (FT Press, 2006). Those books have changed my career.

Hedge fund marketing and sales fee structures vary depending on the type, reputation, and abilities of the third-party marketing (3PM) firm. Some retain only two to three clients at a time and charge retainers for this focus of their attention, while others might work with 10 money managers (clients) at once and only get paid on commission. Usually commissions are 20 percent of both the base fee and performance fee when working with hedge funds.

If you work for a hedge fund, you will be restricted to their strategies, so if their performance dips or the strategy goes out of favor you might not raise any money and it wouldn't be your fault. If you work for a 3PM firm, you would probably get to market two to three different money managers in some capacity across diverse distribution channels such as endowments and foundations, broker-dealers, and directly to high net worth individuals. If a strategy goes out of favor, you just find a new money manager to market as a firm, and you avoid the downside of being a hedge fund sales professional. Common compensation for internal hedge fund salespeople is $80,000 to $200,000 with some making $400,000 to $800,000 per year and maybe three to 10 commissions that might trail off over time. Common compensation for a 3PM, as I mentioned earlier, is a retainer of $60,000 to $150,000 (if they get one) plus 20 percent of fees.

I'm not even 40 years old yet, and I went the third-party marketing route because I want to be able to have knowledge of the DNA and powerful relationships in every major distribution channel, and I want to figure out where the real money and momentum are and be able to shift my focus to that point. I believe it is harder to get a 3PM job because most want you to have a book of business or solid relationships, but it can be done. In my first third-party marketing position I worked for free for three weeks to prove myself, and I took a big cut in pay coming in the door, but it was worth it to learn so much in so little time. Invest in yourself for the long term, never take ethical shortcuts in this industry, and you will do well.

Bonuses of $1,779

The following is a list of book bonuses that we have negotiated or set up on behalf of readers of this book. By purchasing this book you have supported our organization, so in return we would like to provide you with these bonuses.

CHP Designation Tuition Discount: To thank those who have purchased this book, the Hedge Fund Group can offer $100 off registration for the CHP Designation Program when you register for the CHP Level 1 and Level 2 Combination Package on our web site. Registration for the program opens just twice a year, on January 15 and July 15. Learn more at http://HedgeFundCertification.com. **Value of discount: $100.**

InvestorDatabases.com: Fax, e-mail, or mail us a copy of your receipt for purchasing this book and receive 30 percent off your first purchase made at InvestorDatabases.com. Investor Databases provides over a dozen databases that include complete contact details for funds of hedge funds, family offices, wealth management firms, endowment funds, institutional consultants, and more. **Value of discount: $800+.**

HedgeFundPremium.com: Fax, e-mail, or mail us a copy of your receipt for purchasing this book and receive three months' free access to HedgeFundPremium.com and a lifetime membership rate of just $12/month instead of the public price of $27/month. HedgeFundPremium.com is an exclusive membership program for hedge fund professionals. Members gain access to exclusive video content, workbooks, job connector tools, and capital-raising resources. **Value of discount: $200+ (first-year value).**

Hedge Fund Marketing Mechanics: Fax, e-mail, or mail us a copy of your receipt for purchasing this book and receive 40 percent off this package, which provides best practices, overlooked opportunities, strategies, and unique techniques to raise more capital for your hedge fund. Learn more at HedgeFundMarketingMechanics .com. **Value of discount:** $250+ (first-year value).

HedgeFundTraining.com: Fax, e-mail, or mail us a copy of your receipt for purchasing this book and receive $50 off any hedge fund audio program, training session, webinar, seminar, or DVD package. **Value of discount:** $100.

HedgeFundInvestorDirectory.com: Fax, e-mail, or mail us a copy of your receipt for purchasing this book and receive 30 percent off your first purchase made at HedgeFundInvestorDirectory.com. The Hedge Fund Investor Directory was constructed by the Hedge Fund Group, the largest networking association in the hedge fund industry. The Hedge Fund Investor Directory provides contact details for more than 2,000 unique institutions that typically invest in hedge fund managers. Explore the packages we offer at http:// HedgeFundInvestorDirectory/Buy.html. **Value of discount:** $329.

Example Due Diligence Questions

QUESTIONNAIRE

Investment Adviser
Request for Information
A. Corporate Background
1. Name and address of firm.
2. Principal contact.
3. When was your firm founded?
4. Is your firm a registered investment adviser? A commodity trading adviser? A commodity pool operator?
5. Is your firm affiliated with a broker-dealer?
6. What is the organizational structure of your firm?
7. Have there been any material organizational changes in the past five years?
8. What is the current number of employees at your firm? Please provide a breakdown by category.
   a. Portfolio managers: _____
   b. Research analysts: _____
   c. Client services: _____
   d. Administration: _____
   e. Other: _____
9. Please provide a breakdown of your firm's assets under management for the following time periods:

Year	Assets	# Accounts
1992		
1993		
1994		
1995		
1996		
1997		

1998
1999
2000
2001
2002
2003
2004
2005
2006
2007
2008
2009
2010

10. Please list the number of accounts/assets gained/lost during the following periods:

Year	Accounts	Assets	Accounts	Assets
	Gained	Gained	Lost	Lost
1998				
1999				
2000				
2001				
2002				
2003				
2004				
2005				
2006				
2007				
2008				
2009				
2010				

11. Please list all states in which your firm is currently registered to conduct advisory business.

12. What backup technology measures are in place to ensure the integrity of account access and information? What are your disaster retrieval procedures?

    a. Security: _____

    b. Disaster recovery: _____

B. Legal and Compliance

   1. Please detail your firm's fidelity bonding and errors and omissions (E&O) and directors and officers (D&O) coverage (underwriter, limitations, definitions, and claims history).

   2. Please describe all litigation, arbitration, and self-regulatory organization (SRO)/regulatory violations involving the firm, principals, portfolio managers, traders, and any professional support staff in the past 10 years.

   3. Please list all NASD broker-dealers with whom your firm works.

   4. Who has custody of your accounts? Please detail.

   5. What is the procedure for reviewing new accounts?

   6. Describe the flow of client funds from the initial deposit with your firm to the placement at the custodian.

   7. Are regular internal audits performed? If yes, please detail the frequency and process.

   8. Please outline management control procedures.

C. Investment Methodology

   1. Please describe your firm's investment methodology for asset allocation and/or market timing that is utilized by your program.

   2. What technical and/or fundamental indicators does the program utilize? Please provide a description of the portfolio models and indicators tracked.

   3. Please list the asset classes in your investment models.

   4. Are guidelines in place to prevent undue concentrations? If so, please detail.

   5. Describe the process of selecting an investment for use in a model. Does an investment committee review these investments? If yes, who makes up the committee?

   6. How are client risk tolerance and objectives incorporated into the investment decision-making process?

   7. How often is client information updated to ensure that the risk tolerance and objectives are still applicable?

   8. How are buy/sell decisions made?

   9. What factors determine whether an investment is rated aggressive, conservative, and so on?

  10. What resources are devoted to internal research? Are external sources used?

  11. What professional standards are required of the research staff (i.e., experience, CFA, MBA, etc.)?

  12. Describe the frequency and process for adjusting the asset allocation mix. How are these adjustments implemented?

13. Does your firm automatically rebalance portfolios? If so, on what basis?
14. What are the criteria for reallocation and rebalancing a portfolio?
15. Do clients have the option to purchase securities that are not part of the investment model? If so, is this portion of the portfolio segregated?
16. For market timers/asset allocators: How many switches are there in an average year?
17. For private portfolio managers: What is the turnover rate of portfolios? Average number of holdings?
18. What percentage of the time do you anticipate being invested in the markets for each investment discipline managed by your firm?
19. Please detail all changes in investment philosophy since inception.
20. What professional standards are required of your portfolio managers to manage client funds (i.e., experience, CFA, MBA, etc.)?

D. Fee Structure

1. Please describe in detail your fee structure and sharing arrangements, including billing process. Describe your policy concerning working with broker-dealers, as well as your policy relative to representatives or solicitors terminating their relationship with the broker-dealer.
2. Are the fees charged comparable to those charged by similar services?
3. What is the refund policy should a client opt not to continue to employ your services?
4. Please detail all client costs, including transaction fees and custody expenses.
5. Are load funds incorporated in the models, and if so, are the commissions offset?
6. Are direct participation plans utilized in any of these models? If so, how is the market value of these securities valued for purposes of billing?

E. Performance Record

1. Please provide a detailed explanation related to the basis of presentation relative to your performance record. Please ensure that this information addresses the following topics: gross or net of management fees, and actual accounts versus hypothetical. If actual accounts are used, please explain the reason for their inclusion in the composite.

2. Is this performance record the result of any linkage with a prior firm or entity? If yes, provide the date when the current firm's performance begins and any differences between the investment methodologies.

3. Has an independent third party verified your track record? If yes, who?

4. Are the personnel responsible for your performance record still with your firm? If not, how has this affected your firm?

5. Please provide a quarter-by-quarter performance composite (gross and net of advisory fees) for at least 10 years (if available) for your portfolio. Is this composite AIMR compliant? What level of AIMR compliance (Level I or Level II)? Please provide your AIMR disclosure language along with the composite return information.

F. Client Notification

1. Do your statements satisfy ERISA guidelines?

2. Which indexes, if any, are included with the statements?

3. With what frequency are the statements generated?

4. Does your firm provide tax reporting beyond the 1099 reporting provided by the custodian?

Top Hedge Fund Web Sites

Following is a list of top hedge fund and alternative investment web sites run by our team and others that was first published by HedgeFundBlogger .com.

HedgeFundBlogger.com: The number one most popular web site on the topic of hedge funds with over 5,000 free-to-access videos, articles, resources, guides, interviews, and e-books. You may find many resources here that you would have to pay a subscription for elsewhere. (http://HedgeFundBlogger.com)

Albourne Village: Great job board, news feeds, community announcements, and educational white papers as well. This is one of the oldest and most well-rounded web sites in the hedge fund industry. (http://Village.Albourne.com)

HedgeFundsCareer.com: Detailed advice, interviews, Q&A, and training information related to starting and growing a career in the hedge fund industry. (http://HedgeFundsCareer.com)

FINalternatives: Great well-rounded news web site on alternative investments in general. This web site is not exclusively focused on hedge funds, but it does discuss them daily in its original news reports. (www.finalternatives.com)

Hedge Fund Blogspot by Veryan Allen: In-depth analytical takes on recent hedge fund industry trends and challenges. Veryan provides a unique view of the industry as a risk portfolio management consultant. (http://hedgefund.blogspot.com)

SEC Guide to Hedge Funds: A must-read web site for anyone who is starting to complete research on hedge funds as potential investments. (www.sec.gov/answers/hedge.htm)

ThirdPartyMarketing.com: The only free-to-access educational web site on capital raising, fund marketing, and third-party marketing that provides consulting advice to both marketers and fund managers. The web site hosts over 250 resources, articles, and videos. (http://ThirdPartyMarketing.com)

New York Times **DealBook: Hedge Funds:** This blog is hosted by the *New York Times* and covers developing hedge fund stories each day. Great place to get some insight and opinion on top of the regular news. (http://dealbook.blogs.nytimes.com/category/hedge-funds/)

Hedge Fund Startup Guru.com: Articles and videos for emerging hedge fund managers, new hedge fund start-ups, and traders who are considering launching a new fund. (http://HedgeFundStartupGuru.com)

Investopedia on Hedge Funds: This web site provides over a dozen educational articles of more than 800 words each on hedge funds. It reads like a short magazine on long-term hedge fund industry facts, statistics, and trends. (www.investopedia.com/terms/h/hedgefund.asp)

Family Offices Group: The educational web site of the largest family office networking association in the wealth management industry. It contains over 500 articles and videos on family offices. (http://FamilyOfficesGroup.com)

Hedge Funds Research Guide, Harvard Baker Library: A great resource put together by Harvard University on hedge funds. It is a bit dated now but still holds valuable leads to additional resources. (www.library.hbs.edu/guides/hedgefunds/index_print.html)

HedgeFundMessageBoard.com: Industry forum for hedge fund professionals and hedge fund managers. (http://HedgeFundMessageBoard.com)

PrimeBrokerageGuide.com: The number one web site on the hedge fund prime brokerage niche industry. (http://primebrokerageguide.com)

Glossary

$\mathbf{F}$ollowing is a list of top hedge fund and alternative investment terms and keywords that are important to understand if you are going to work in the hedge fund industry.

alpha   Alpha goes a step further than excess return and adds risk to the equation. Alpha is the portfolio's risk-adjusted performance or the "value added" provided by a manager. Mathematically, alpha is the incremental difference between a manager's actual results and his expected results, given the level of risk. A positive alpha indicates that a portfolio has produced returns above the expected level—at the same level of risk—and a negative alpha suggests the portfolio underperformed given the level of risk assumed.

back office   The back office staff deal with trade processing, reconciliation, and cash management. They also perform administrative functions that support the trading of securities, including record keeping, trade confirmation, trade settlement, and regulatory compliance. If used in sales, the back office fulfills customers' orders and may usually perform the duties involved in customer support call centers.

beta   Beta is a measure of sensitivity to the market benchmark, or how volatile a security or portfolio is relative to the whole market. A diversified portfolio with a beta of 1.0 would indicate that the portfolio would respond in tandem with the market. A beta greater than 1.0 indicates that a portfolio would be more responsive to market movements, while a beta below 1.0 would indicate a muted response. Aggressive investors may choose portfolios with higher betas, while defensive investors may focus on low-beta investments.

broker   A broker acts as an agent or intermediary for a buyer and a seller. The buyer, seller, and broker may all be individuals, or one or more may be a business or other institution. For example, a stockbroker works for a brokerage firm and handles client orders to buy or sell stocks, bonds, commodities, and options in return for a commission or asset-based fee. A floor broker handles buy and sell orders on the floor of a securities or commodities exchange. A real estate broker represents the seller in a real estate transaction and receives a commission on the sale.

buy side   The buy side consists of institutional investors, which includes insurance companies, mutual funds, pension funds, endowment funds, and hedge funds. The buy side refers to firms that buy and sell as customers of these market makers, usually taking speculative positions or making relative value trades.

Calmar and Sterling ratios   Calmar and Sterling ratios are well suited for presenting the worst-case picture since they take into account maximum drawdown—that is, the worst possible losing streak. This feature causes them to be used extensively in hedge fund applications.

capital introduction services   This is a process whereby the prime broker attempts to introduce its hedge fund clients to qualified hedge fund investors who have an interest in exploring new opportunities to make hedge fund investments.

chief compliance officer (CCO)   A CCO is primarily responsible for overseeing and managing compliance issues in an organization. The responsibilities of the position often include leading enterprise compliance efforts; designing and implementing internal controls, policies, and procedures to assure compliance with applicable local, state, and federal laws and regulations and third-party guidelines; managing audits and investigations into regulatory and compliance issues; and responding to requests for information from regulatory bodies.

clearing   Clearing denotes all activities from the time a commitment is made for a transaction until it is settled. It involves the management of post-trading, presettlement credit exposures to ensure that trades are settled in accordance with market rules, even if a buyer or seller should become insolvent prior to settlement.

Commodities and Futures Trading Commission (CFTC)   The Commodities and Futures Trading Commission (CFTC) is an independent agency of the U.S. government. The main objectives of the CFTC are to protect market users and the public from fraud, manipulation, and abusive practices related to the sale of commodity and financial futures and options; and to foster open, competitive, and financially sound futures and option markets.

custodian   A custodian is a financial institution responsible for safeguarding a firm's or individual's financial assets. The role of a custodian in such a case would be the following: to hold in safekeeping assets such as equities and bonds, arrange settlement of any purchases and sales of such securities, collect information on and income from such assets, provide information on the underlying companies and their annual general meetings, manage cash transactions, perform foreign exchange transactions where required, and provide regular reporting on all their activities to their clients.

dark pool   Dark pools offer institutional investors liquidity that is not displayed on order books. This is useful for traders who wish to move large numbers of shares without revealing themselves to the open market.

dealer   A dealer is an individual or a firm that buys assets for and sells assets from its own portfolio, as opposed to bringing buyers and sellers together. Dealers, or principals, buy and sell securities for their own accounts, adding liquidity to the marketplace and seeking to profit from the spread between the prices at which they buy and sell. Dealers are sometimes able to offer investors better prices, but they may tend to make recommendations based on their own ownership positions.

drawdown   A drawdown is measured from the time a retrenchment begins to when a new high is reached. This method is used because a valley can't be measured until a new high occurs. Once the new high is reached, the percentage change from the old high to the smallest trough is recorded. Drawdowns help determine an investment's financial risk. An analyst can use this as a tool to compare a security's possible reward to its risk.

execution   Execution is the act of filling an order to buy or sell a security. That is, when a broker executes an order, he actually makes a trade on behalf of the client. The date of execution is known as the trade date.

front office   The front office deals with the positioning of trade, hedging, and value at risk (VAR). The primary objective is to trade actively and manage liquidity.

fund administration services   Fund administration services are a set of activities that are carried out in support of the actual process of running a hedge fund. Services include the calculation of the net asset value (NAV), including the calculation of the fund's income and expense accruals, preparation of semiannual and annual accounts, maintenance of the fund's financial books and records, payment of the fund's expenses, and supervision of the orderly liquidation and dissolution of the fund.

fund of hedge funds   A fund of hedge funds is an investment company that invests in hedge funds rather than in individual securities. Some funds of hedge funds register their securities with the SEC. These funds of hedge funds must provide investors with a prospectus and must file certain reports quarterly with the SEC. They hold a diversified portfolio of generally uncorrelated hedge funds that may be widely diversified or focused on a specific sector or geographical location.

hedge fund   Hedge funds pool the investors' money and invest in financial instruments in order to make positive returns. They pursue absolute returns on their underlying instruments. Every hedge fund has its own investment strategy that determines the type of investments and the methods of investment it undertakes. There are over 14 different investment strategies in which hedge funds invest, and each has its own risk and return. Hedge funds, as a class, invest in a broad range of investments including shares, debt, and commodities. They are able to take speculative positions in derivative securities such as options and have the ability to short-sell stocks. This will typically increase the leverage—and thus the risk—of the fund. This also means that it's possible for hedge funds to make money when the market is falling. Hedge funds are only available to a specific group of sophisticated investors with high net worth. The U.S. government deems them "accredited investors," and the criteria for becoming one are lengthy and restrictive.

high-water mark   A hedge fund applies a high-water mark to an investor's money; this means that the manager will only receive performance fees on that particular pool of invested money when its current value is greater than its previous greatest value. If the investment drops in value, then the manager must bring it back above the previous greatest value before he can receive performance fees again.

hurdle rate   The hurdle rate is an established minimum return that an investor's investment must earn to the application of performance/incentive fees.

kurtosis   The scaled fourth power of observations in the tail distribution is kurtosis. The classical interpretation of kurtosis is that it measures both peakedness and tail heaviness of a distribution relative to that of the normal distribution. Consequently, its use is restricted to symmetric distributions. A high kurtosis portrays a chart with fat tails and a low, even distribution, whereas a low kurtosis portrays a chart with skinny tails and a distribution concentrated toward the mean. It is also called the volatility of volatility.

leverage   Leverage is the extent to which a fund is utilizing borrowed money. A highly leveraged fund or company is considered a risky investment because it might not find lenders in the future. Leverage is not always bad, however; it can make both gains and losses much more extreme than otherwise possible.

management fee   The management fee is calculated as a percentage of a fund's net asset value. The fee may range from 1 to 4 percent, but 2 percent is the standard figure. This is the fee intended to compensate the managers for professionally managing the investor's assets.

omega   The omega measure provides the information about benchmark returns that is relevant in the tail of the distribution curve. Omega calculations involve a complicated framework, but it captures all the information about portfolio returns and expresses it in a manner that is intuitive from an investment performance viewpoint.

performance fee   The performance fee or incentive fee is calculated as a percentage of the fund's profit, considering both realized and unrealized gains. Typically the fund manager charges 20 percent of the returns as a performance fee.

prime brokerage   This is a package of services offered by the investment banks to the hedge funds. The advantage that a hedge fund enjoys is that the prime broker provides a centralized securities clearing facility for the hedge fund, and the hedge fund's collateral requirements are netted across all deals handled by the prime broker. The prime broker in turn benefits by earning fees on financing the client's long and short cash and security positions, and by charging, in some cases, fees for clearing and/or other services.

redemptions   Redemptions are withdrawals from hedge funds by investors which are sometimes subject to lock-up periods, gating clauses, or other terms.

risk budgeting   Risk budgeting is the process of decomposing the aggregate risk of a portfolio into its constituents on a quantitative basis; setting risk limits to each asset class, factor, and/or investment manager; allocating assets in compliance with risk budgets; monitoring the use or abuse of risk budgets on an ongoing basis; analyzing the results; and improving the investment process.

Securities and Exchange Commission (SEC)   The U.S. Securities and Exchange Commission (SEC) exists to protect investors; to maintain fair, orderly, and efficient markets; and to facilitate capital formation.

sell side   Banks and brokers are the main constituents of the sell side. The term refers to firms that take orders from buy side firms and then work the orders. Sell side firms are paid through commissions charged on the sales price of the stock. Sell side firms employ research analysts, traders, and salespeople who collectively strive to generate ideas and execute trades for buy side firms, enticing them to do business.

Sharpe ratio   The Sharpe ratio considers total risk and is more suitable for diversified portfolios. The ratio is most commonly used because it has desirable properties, such as proportionality to the *t*-statistic (for returns in excess of zero) and the centrality of the Sharpe ratio squared to optimal portfolio allocation. But the ratio is leverage invariant and does not incorporate correlations and risks involving higher movements.

short-sell Short-selling is the sale of a security that the seller does not own, or a sale that is completed by the delivery of a security borrowed by the seller. Short-sellers assume that they will be able to buy the stock at a lower amount than the price at which they sold short. Short-sellers make money if the stock price goes down.

soft dollar A soft dollar payment is a payment made by institutional investment funds to their service providers. Usually soft dollars are incorporated into brokerage fees, and the expenses they pay for may not be reported directly.

Sortino ratio The Sortino ratio adjusts by drawdown. The ratio does not consider up movements in volatility but only underperformance and some threshold of MAR. Sortino can look deceptively high/favorable (upon trend reversal) if the ex-post estimation is based on a period of upwardly trending returns, since downside deviation underestimates the two-sided risk if the estimation period is not long enough to include loss periods.

standard deviation The standard deviation is often used by investors to measure the risk of a stock or a stock portfolio. The basic idea is that the standard deviation is a measure of volatility: The more a stock's returns vary from the stock's average return, the more volatile the stock.

third-party marketing Third-party marketing, in the context of a hedge fund definition, refers to a set of sales and marketing services offered to hedge fund managers by specialized marketing firms. Provided services may include the production of marketing materials such as pamphlets and spreadsheets, the management of advertising in media, analyzing investment market statistics, and customer relations management. The role of third-party marketing firms is to serve as a bridge between fund managers and potential investors. Third-party marketing firms can offer recommendations; contact assistance; and comparative ratings of hedge fund risk ratings, performance in the market, and fee structures.

The types of services that hedge fund third-party marketing firms offer can include:

- Fully outsourced marketing and sales services.
- Channel or geographically specific marketing efforts.
- Creation of marketing materials including a full PowerPoint presentation and one-page marketing piece.
- Assistance in developing a standard request for proposal (RFP) and populating major hedge fund databases.
- Representation at industry social events, conferences, and private dinner parties.
- Advice on how best to move forward in a diverse range of capital-raising channels.
- Public relations and media consultation as needed.

There are as many types of third-party marketing agreements in the hedge fund industry as there are third-party marketers, but most of the value provided to hedge fund clients is through one of the activities just listed.

Treynor ratio The Treynor ratio considers only systematic risk and is used for less diversified portfolios or single securities. As a market-neutral hedge fund approaches beta neutrality, the Treynor ratio approaches infinity. Hence, for market-neutral funds, the Treynor ratio is not used. As such, the Treynor ratio is not chosen for hedge fund ranking or comparisons.

value at risk (VAR) Value at risk (VAR) measures the worst expected loss under normal market conditions over a specific time interval at a given confidence level. Another way of expressing this is that VAR is the lowest quartile of the potential losses that can occur in a given portfolio during a specified time period.

About the Author

Richard Wilson is a hedge fund consultant, capital raiser, and adviser who has directly raised over $230 million. Mr. Wilson runs the 35,000-member Hedge Fund Group, which runs the Certified Hedge Fund Professional (CHP) Designation Program. He also runs the number one most popular web site on hedge funds, HedgeFundBlogger.com. Often speaking at conferences in locations such as New York, Brussels, Moscow, and São Paulo, Richard's firm helps hedge fund managers raise more capital and train hedge fund employees on hedge fund fundamentals.

Mr. Wilson's education includes a bachelor's degree in business administration with special projects in systems thinking, an MBA in marketing, and training coursework at Harvard University ALM Program on the psychology of influence and persuasion. In addition to this text, Richard Wilson published *Rainmaker* and the *Hedge Fund Blog Book* in 2008, a popular e-book on hedge funds which has been downloaded over 100,000 times.

Index

Institutional investment consultants, 138
Institutionalization:
  Bob Pardo on, 19–21
  Eric Warshal on, 30–32
  Hendrik Klein on, 26–29
  Lance Baraker and William Katts on,
    32–36
  Nakul, Nayyar on, 24–26
  overview, 17–18
  Sheri Kanesaka on, 30–32
  Stephen Abrahams on, 18–19
  Vinod Paul on, 21–24
Internships, 157, 158
Investment Management Consultants
    Association (IMCA), 95
Investment process, 145
Investopedia on Hedge Funds, 178
Investordatabases.com, 169
Investor relationship management (IRM),
    143–144
Investors, categories of, 147–148
Israel, Samuel III, 103–104

Jaeger, Robert, 163
Janus Capital, 151
Jones, Alfred, 8

Kanesaka, Sheri, 29–30
Katts, William, 32–36
Klein, Hendrik, 26–29, 59–60
Koenig, David, 130–133
Kovner, Bruce, 87

Learning strategies, 139
Legal and compliance firms, 11
Liquidity, 6, 7
Lock-up period, 6, 7
Long Term Capital Management (LTCM),
    102–103
Long-term strategies, 110–111

Madoff, Bernard L., 104–105
Madoff Effect, 69
Main, Andrew, 124–130
Management fees, 132–133
Marketing, 21, 23, 39–61
  cold-calling, 152–153
  compensation for, 152
  educational, 42–43
  e-mail, 45–49

  to financial advisors vs. family offices,
    148–149
  for giant hedge funds, 110
  importance of marketing materials, 99
  public relations management, 41–42, 49
  smaller funds, 40
  in start-up phase, 80
  third-party, more
  top 10 mistakes, 47–49
  See also Third-party marketers/marketing
Media, and hedge funds, 9–10
Mentors, 157
Meriwether, John, 102
Michelman & Robinson, LLP, 29
Multi-prime brokerage models, 12
Multistrategy hedge funds, 138

Nayyar, Nakul, 24–26, 86–89
Networking, 142, 154, 166–167
New York Times Dealbook: Hedge Funds,
    178
Nonexecutive advisory boards, 129
Nummi, Rick, 65–71

Operations improvement, 32–36
  See also Institutionalization
Options, 88
Orienting reflex, 141–142
Outside resource use, 12
Outsourcing, 20, 31, 34

Pagan, Eben, 2–3
Pardo, Bob, 19–21
Pardo Capital Limited, 19
Paul, Vinod, 21–24
Pedigree, 67–68, 72, 110, 145
Performance fees, 132–133
Pitch book, 80–81
Powell, Thomas, 72–73
PowerPoint presentations, 78–79, 81,
    144–145
PrimeBrokerageGuide.com, 178
Prime brokers, 10
Private company investing, 143
Process documentation, 34–35, 140
Professional training programs, 156–157
Proprietary trading, 86
Providers of hedge funds, 10–11
Public relations, 41–42, 49, 150

Contact the Author

If you would like to contact Richard Wilson, offer any feedback, or share thoughts on potentially working together, please use the contact details below to get in touch.

E-Mail

Richard@HedgeFundGroup.org

CHP Designation Support E-Mail

Team@HedgeFundCertification.com

Mailing Address

Hedge Fund Group (HFG)

3300 NW 185th Avenue, Suite 108

Portland, Oregon 97229

Over the past two years our company has sent and received over 800,000 e-mails, and we have had to stop publishing our phone number to the public to make sure our current clients are served well. Please touch base over e-mail first if you have any feedback or questions.